THE ETHICS OF CONFLICTS OF INTEREST IN BUSINESS

On Ethics and Economics

Series Editor: Mark D. White, Professor and Chair, Department of
Philosophy, College of Staten Island, CUNY

"On Ethics and Economics" explores the ethical aspects of topics tradi-
tionally studied through economics. Starting from the position that no
economic issue should be examined in an ethical vacuum, books in the
series will feature philosophers, economists and other scholars exploring
ethics behind issues normally treated as primarily economic in nature.
Titles will explore the implicit ethical assumptions made when discussing issues and propose alternative ethical foundations for them, as well as
investigating ethical aspects of issues that are often neglected.

Titles in the Series:

THE ETHICS OF CONFLICTS OF INTEREST IN BUSINESS

AN INTRODUCTION

Alonso Villarán

ROWMAN & LITTLEFIELD
Lanham • Boulder • New York • London

Credits and acknowledgments for material borrowed from other sources, and reproduced with permission, appear on the appropriate page within the text.

Published by Rowman & Littlefield
An imprint of The Rowman & Littlefield Publishing Group, Inc.
4501 Forbes Boulevard, Suite 200, Lanham, Maryland 20706
www.rowman.com

British Library Cataloguing in Publication Information Available

Library of Congress Cataloging-in-Publication Data Is Available

ISBN: 978-1-78661-611-1 (cloth : alk. paper)
ISBN: 978-1-78661-612-8 (pbk. : alk. paper)
ISBN: 978-1-78661-613-5 (electronic)

♾™ The paper used in this publication meets the minimum requirements of American National Standard for Information Sciences—Permanence of Paper for Printed Library Materials, ANSI/NISO Z39.48-1992.

CONTENTS

ACKNOWLEDGMENTS

Many thanks to the authorities and my colleagues at *Universidad del Pacífico* (Lima, Perú). Without their support, this book would not exist.

I owe gratitude as well, to the people at *Rowman & Littlefield*, especially Mark D. White, Dhara Snowden, Rebecca Anastasi, Isobel Cowper-Coles, Scarlet Furness, Kym Lyons, Hannah Fisher, Frankie Mace, and everyone else involved in the project.

I am indebted to Thomas L. Carson, who casually introduced me to the topic several years ago (and who reviewed some of the material). Michael Davis and John Boatright, who at some point helped me get some of the core literature (and taught me a lot about conflicts of interest through their writings) are also due many thanks. I appreciate as well the anonymous reviewers who commented on the chapter sample. I must also gratefully acknowledge Kenneth Hermse who copyedited the manuscript. Many thanks are also in order for my research assistant, Jean Christian Egoávil, who helped me with this project since day one. Thanks as well to James Spence, for receiving me at the *Great Lakes Philosophy Conference* and encouraging me to write the book.

My sincere thanks, finally, to my wife Laura for her reviews, support, and advise.

INTRODUCTION

Has anyone ever stolen your lunch, drink, or snack at work? Or have you ever stolen someone else's lunch, drink, or snack?

According to a survey by BusinessWire from 2017, one in every five workers admitted having eaten someone else's lunch, drink, or snack out of the fridge.[1] The way some of the victims confront this situation can be hilarious. My favorite is K. Farrel's story, as reported by the BBC:

> I had to laugh when someone I used to work with opened the fridge with everyone in the canteen and said "Oh no! That had my medication in it! If any of you have drank my milk, you'd better phone your doctor." Then just walked out. I found it hilarious because I knew he'd made it up. But there were some very worried people in there.[2]

The ethics of this form of fighting office food theft is a topic in itself—as is the ethics of putting laxatives in the soon-to-be stolen food and drinks, which is what other victims do. Analyzing this (as well as the ethics of stealing), though, would lead us astray.

Why am I speaking of this in the first place, then? Because it allows me to make a basic distinction that will lead us to the topic of this book, which is the ethics of conflicts of interest in business.

Ask yourself: do office food thieves face conflicts of interest when they are tempted to grab the cookie or the can of cola? What about those tempted to cheat on their spouses with a colleague? Or those tempted to lie to their coworkers about their weekend whereabouts? Do they face conflicts of interest?

These are not conflicts of interest. They are ordinary moral problems in the workplace. And this is the distinction: conflicts of interest, being moral problems, have something special about them, i.e., something that sets them apart from ordinary moral problems. Otherwise, we would not have given them a special name. So, what is it that distinguishes one from the other? Well, making that distinction is part of the burden of this book.

Now, I am sure you are not reading this book to distinguish ordinary moral problems in business from conflicts of interest. You are here because you want to know more about conflicts of interest—or, of course, because you are a student and your professor chose the topic and perhaps even assigned the book. If your case is the latter, then I need to attract your interest with a stronger reason.

The reason is simple: if you work or will soon work for a living, a conflict of interest is coming your way (and will be followed by more). Will you be prepared for that? Will you be ready to identify it and to manage it properly? Also, you might eventually, if not already, lead a business or an organization. Do you have a sufficient grasp to regulate them properly? This book will help you with all this and a little more—all as part of the price.

As a book on the ethics of conflict of interest, this book would be incomplete, even groundless, if it did not introduce ethics to readers. This, in fact, will be the focus of chapter 1. More specifically, in the chapter, I will introduce readers to, or reinforce their knowledge of, a central concept in ethics—the moral law—from the perspective of the two most influential moral theories of the last 250 years or so: Immanuel Kant's deontology and John S. Mill's utilitarianism. In the chapter, I will also reveal the structure of moral problems in general, which will help us in defining conflicts of interest and distinguishing them from regular moral problems.

Now that we have a basic idea of ethics, in chapter 2, I will discuss business ethics in the most popular language of business ethics: that of corporate social responsibility. Now, as with ethics, it would be impossible to cover all the theories and all the debate around the topic within the confines of a single chapter. Because of this, in the chapter I will focus on two of the most influential versions of corporate social responsibility: R. Edward Freeman's (so-called) stakeholder theory and Milton Friedman's (so-called) stock or shareholder theory. I will then analyze the relationship between corporate social responsibility and conflicts of interest and argue for a need to devote more time and resources to the latter.

Having touched on ethics, corporate social responsibility, and the relationship between corporate social responsibility and conflicts of interest in business ethics, in chapter 3, I will finally move on to conflicts of interest per se. More specifically, I will tackle the preliminary question: What is a conflict of interest? This will be an opportunity to summon the philosophical champions of conflicts of interest, compare how they define conflicts of interest, and take a position. Of course, you may not agree with this position, but you will definitively leave the chapter with a good idea of what a conflict of interest is—and thus be better equipped to identify them when they cross your path.

A definition, though, is not enough to master their identification. For this, a typology is also necessary. In fact, without a typology or classification, we risk failure to spot a whole class of conflicts of interest: the intrinsic type, paradigmatically, as we will see. But the chapter is worth writing for its own sake. In fact, not writing it would equate to writing a book on, say, dogs, that overlooked their breeds. Would not this limit our understanding of these animals in a substantial way?

In chapter 5, I will tackle the morally problematic nature of conflicts of interest. Why are they morally problematic and not, say, merely legally problematic? Conflicts of interest are morally problematic for several reasons, but I will highlight a fundamental one—one related to promises. After clarifying and explaining this, I will analyze promises from deontological and utilitarian perspectives (building upon the introduction to these perspectives in chapter 1). The point of all this is to make absolutely plain why conflicts of interest should be taken seriously.

Those who are more practically oriented will find special joy in chapter 6, which is devoted to the proper management of conflicts of interest. What should we do when we encounter one, or even before we encounter one? In this chapter, I will address this question at the individual and at organizational levels, discussing measures that range from exploring how conflicts of interests are regulated at our work or by our professions (first individual measure) to regulating them through codes of ethics (last organizational measure). The talk on conflicts of interest will, in turn, leave us in a perfect position for the next, and final topic: conflicts of interest in codes of ethics.

In chapter 7, the last before the conclusion, I will analyze the ways conflicts of interests are regulated in the business world. We will put everything we have learned in previous chapters to use here. We will see the different ways in which major codes of ethics (those of some of the biggest corporations) fail—through flawed definitions, important omissions, and incomplete management measures, among other flaws. The purpose, though, is not merely to criticize for criticism's sake. The real intention is to gather the most common errors so readers with the power to rectify, draft, or commission a code of ethics do not commit them. Even if you do not have that power now, or do not plan to have it in the future, the chapter will strengthen your brand-new mastery of conflicts of interest.

Now, some clarifications. First, this is a book on the *ethics* of conflicts of interest in business, but on ethics in a narrow or strict sense. In other words, it is grounded in moral philosophy. This clarification refers not only to the moral theories that I will introduce in chapter 1 (Kant's deontology and Mill's utilitarianism) but to the literature on conflicts itself. In other words, when defining and classifying (and so on) conflicts of interest, the book will engage with the philosophical literature on the topic, i.e., with what philosophers like Michael Davis and Thomas L. Carson have said about it. The literature, though, transcends philosophy and so one can find lawyers, physicians, etcetera analyzing conflicts of interest in their respective fields. Everyone is welcome and encouraged to search for these publications.

Second, this is a book on the ethics of conflicts of interest in *business*, but people from other professions can learn from it as well. The examples throughout the book will be taken, or imagined, from the business world. Still, the definition, the classification, the assessment, the management, and even the analysis of the way conflicts of interest are regulated in business codes of ethics can be easily applied to other fields.

Third, this is a book on the ethics of *conflicts of interest* in business, but it is, more broadly speaking, a book on business ethics as well. Why am I saying this? Because conflicts of interest are at the heart of business ethics. No other topic in business ethics cuts through the heart of business ethics as conflicts of interest does. Advertising ethics, financial ethics, accounting ethics, etcetera—all these specialized areas of business ethics only appeal to the advertiser, the financial agent, the accountant, etcetera. Conflicts of interest, on the other hand, appeals to anyone involved in business. You may contest: "What about corporate social responsibility?" To that, I will answer: it may be cross-cutting but, as I will make plain in chapter 3, it is an elitist way to do business ethics. Conflicts of interest, on the other hand, is both cross-cutting and egalitarian.

Ethics, business ethics, and conflicts of interest are all fascinating topics. It is time to discuss each one of them, in that same order.

Chapter 1

ETHICS AND THE MORAL LAW

Perhaps the most popular moral question among businesspeople is whether ethics is profitable. This is not surprising. After all, usually businesspeople get into business for money. Advocates of business ethics and corporate social responsibility know this well, which motivates them to highlight the many ways in which ethics is a "good investment"—a way of doing business that pays off.

The question of the profitability of ethics is part of a bigger one that philosophers have asked for millennia: Is ethics the path to happiness? One can trace this question back to Plato, who spends much of *The Republic* trying to convince us, against popular opinion, that this is indeed the case.

This will not, though, be our main concern. Instead, we will try to answer a more basic question: What does it mean to be ethical? After all, the main reason we are gathered around this book is to analyze the ethics of conflicts of interest (to unveil their essence, moral status, etcetera). Happiness will be part of our discussion, but mainly as a duty instead of as a reward for doing what ethics commands.

So what does it mean to be ethical? Being ethical means following the moral law and the duties that flow from it. Now, I will not be surprised if this answer leaves some readers perplexed. After all, the moral law is a somewhat forgotten concept in our times. Pay attention to the words people use in ordinary moral discussions—those that take place in living rooms and op-eds. Is the moral law even alluded to? Words like "rights," "values," and "tolerance" prevail instead. The fact is that without the moral law, these and other precious things would have no ground—an insight that most of the greatest premodern and modern moral philosophers (i.e., those before Friedrich Nietzsche) knew very well.

1

This foundational chapter, then, will be devoted to the moral law. To make the reason for this completely clear, the moral law will open the door to an understanding of ethics, which will in turn open the door to an understanding of the ethics of conflicts of interests.

A few lines above I mentioned the commitment of premodern and modern moral philosophers to the moral law. It would be quite interesting to unpack that history, i.e., the history of the moral law in philosophy, but that would be too indulgent in a book like this. Instead, we will focus on two of the most influential versions of the moral law nowadays: Immanuel Kant's deontology (mainly as presented in his *Grounding for the Metaphysics of Morals*) and John S. Mill's utilitarianism (mainly as expounded in his *Utilitarianism*).

The influence of the moral law, it is worth clarifying, is not explicit—if it were, the moral law would be a popular concept. Still, the ideals that these versions of the moral law contain are certainly part of the "spirit of our times," even if we do not recognize their source. In fact, after this chapter is over, readers will feel that what they learned was in some mysterious way something they already knew.

With regard to the moral law, we will discuss three things: its source (Where does it come from?), its formulation (What does it command?), and its importance (Why does it matter?). We will start chronologically, with Kant, but switch to Mill (as well as switching questions) when convenient.

A final clarification before we depart. Without denying the many differences between Kant's deontology and Mill's utilitarianism, the approach that follows will not be confrontational. Instead, I will do everything in my power, after presenting what they say about the moral law, to highlight some of the insights that unite them—with the intention of summoning them for our future efforts to master conflicts of interest.

A CATEGORICAL IMPERATIVE FROM REASON: THE MORAL LAW'S SOURCE IN KANT

"Everything in nature works according to laws,"[1] asserts Kant, and there seems to be nothing controversial about this. After all, we are all subject to the natural laws that govern the universe. Thus, if we jump from a building, we fall—and, most probably, die. Kant, though, prepares the ground for a bolder thesis: that, as rational beings, we humans have the power to think and act in accordance to laws that spring from reason.

So far so good, but there is a problem. Humans are not in fact purely rational, so we sometimes—more often than we like to admit—disregard rational laws. This is why such laws manifest themselves to us as commands or imperatives that express an ought: "do this"; "do not do that."

The laws or imperatives to which we are referring, Kant expands, are of two types: hypothetical and categorical. A hypothetical imperative is one that tells us what to do to attain something we may or do desire. For instance, there is a hypothetical imperative that holds: "If you want to boil water, bring it to 212 degrees Fahrenheit." Now, right now I do not want to boil water, so I do not consider myself compelled to do what this hypothetical imperative commands. But the next time I want to boil water (and most probably that time will come), I will follow the imperative more closely. It would be the rational thing to do if I wanted to, say, boil an egg.

Through hypothetical imperatives, then, reason orients us toward the attainment of our mundane goals: boiling water, creating a marketing plan, and even—to speak of that which we all naturally desire—attaining happiness. In these cases, reason (informed by experience) tells us "If you want to create a marketing plan, describe your target audience," "If you want to be happy (and believe that happiness requires financial peace), save for your retirement," etcetera. If you want X, do Y. *If you.*

At this level, reason is instrumental. We have wants, and reason tells us how to fulfill them. Make no mistake: this is something to be grateful for. But reason is not merely instrumental. Reason is more than a tool at the service of our desires. Reason is the source of a higher order—an imperative that tells us, without an "if" or a condition, how to act morally. I am talking about the categorical imperative; the "If you want X" disappears from the equation. We simply must "do Y" (soon we will specify the "Y"). This applies whether we like it or not.

As we can see, the main difference between a hypothetical and the categorical imperative is the unconditional nature of what the latter orders. Hypothetical imperatives are interested imperatives: if we follow them, we will get what we want (whether we should not want what we want is another question; sometimes we are better off not getting what we want, as experienced people know). The categorical imperative, on the other hand, is disinterested. It does not promise anything and frequently even comes at a high price—namely, our own prosperity. The categorical imperative is the voice of our own reason telling us how to lead, more than a happy life, a moral one.

But how does this relate to the moral law? Well, the moral law *is* the categorical imperative that flows from reason to tell us what our moral duties are and thus how to become good. This is something, according to Kant, that no philosopher saw before—and that explains why "all [of them and their theories] had to fail."[2] Others did speak of the moral law, but no one saw it as a law that springs from our own reason, or that what it orders it does so categorically. But what does the moral law, the supreme principle of morality, command? Its categorical nature opens the door to its formulation.

TEXT BOX 1.1: IMMANUEL KANT

Such an extraordinary philosopher must have had an exciting life, right? So where to begin?

With Kant, though, the question is: Can we even begin? Is there anything worth sharing, besides his place of birth (Königsberg, Prussia) and the years he walked the Earth (1724–1804)? The fact is that—as Heine puts it—"the life story of Immanuel Kant is difficult to describe, because he had neither a life, nor a story."[33]

True. Kant did not have, on the face of it, a very exciting life. He did not fight a war (unlike Socrates), did not have unconditional lovers (unlike Socrates), and was not unjustly condemned to death for thinking (unlike Socrates). The great German philosopher never left his hometown, never dated anyone, and died a peaceful death.

That said, it must have been very exciting to author some of the most influential books ever written: *Critique of Pure Reason*, *Critique of Practical Reason*, *Critique of Judgment*, among others. It must have been even more exciting to address, in those books, life's most important questions: What can I know? What should I do? What may I hope?

In writing those books and addressing these questions, Kant was, literally, changing the world. In short, he arguably abolished metaphysics, launched a groundbreaking formalist ethics, called for more morals and less ritual in religion, and conceived of what we now know as the United Nations, etcetera.

When they say he lived an unexciting life, therefore, we should protest, or at least qualify: would you too not hold yourself back from some excesses and dramas if, in exchange, you gained insights that, to this day, remain hidden? (You do not have to answer those questions. My point is that Kant did live a highly exciting intellectual life.)

Hence, the best place to start with getting to know Kant is his own philosophy and, when it comes to his moral philosophy, the moral law is at the heart of it.

RESPECT HUMANITY! KANT'S VERSION
OF THE MORAL LAW

What can the moral law (our highest duty) order us to do so categorically, disinterestedly? According to Kant, the following: "Act only according to that maxim whereby you can at the same time will that it should become a universal law."[4] This highly abstract formula, known as the "formula of universal law," needs clarification.

The key concept to begin understanding this formula is that of maxims. According to Kant, behind our actions are maxims or "subjective [personal] principles of volition"[5] that explain those same actions. For example, I am usually on time for my meetings. If someone asks why, the answer is that I live by the maxim: "Every time I have an appointment, I will be on time." The problem is that not all maxims are moral. Immoral maxims, in turn, condition unethical behavior. That is why we need to test the morality of our maxims and get rid of the bad ones. The way to do so is through a universality test—a three-step moral test.

The three steps (implicit in the formula) are the following: (1) Identify the maxim at play; (2) Paraphrase the maxim as if it were valid for everyone, i.e., as if it were a universal law; and (3) Ask yourself if you can will both the maxim and the universalized version. If you cannot, then the maxim and the corresponding action are immoral.

Let's further analyze how this works (and how we can derive more concrete, "secondary" moral duties from the moral law) with one of Kant's own examples: the lying promise. Someone is tempted to make a lying promise, but wonders whether doing so is ethical.

The maxim can be phrased as follows: "Whenever I am under financial stress, I will ask for a loan with a lying promise of repaying it." (The form of the maxim can be established as follows: "Whenever A happens, I will do B." Do not confuse a maxim with a hypothetical imperative, which has the form "If you want X, do Y.")

The universalized version of the maxim, in turn, is: "Whenever someone is under financial stress, he or she will ask for a loan with a lying promise of repaying it."

Now for the analysis, it is impossible (contradictory) to will both the maxim and its universalized version. If one wills to make a lying promise when under financial stress, one cannot (coherently) will a universal law of lying promises. Why? Because if lying promises became universal, nobody would believe in promises and they (as in loans) would cease to exist. To will the universalized version of the maxim is to will the end of promises and loans, and thus the end of the maxim. To express this in reverse, to will the maxim is to will promises and loans and thus not the maxim's universalized version. Now, since it is impossible to will the maxim and its universalized version, the maxim is immoral and it needs to be outlawed.

As Kant further explains, when we consider doing something immoral, we never will the universalization of our maxim (that is, again, impossible). Instead, we will the universalization of the opposite of the maxim—namely, truthful promises, and make an "exception to the law for ourselves."[6] We play dirty, break rules that we otherwise support.

I mentioned that this moral test allows us not only to check our maxims but also to derive secondary moral duties (the moral law being our "primary" duty). In our example, the stated duty is not to make lying promises, but of course there are more. Other duties that Kant develops are those of not committing suicide, cultivating one's talents, and benefiting others. We will return to the secondary duties of morality later.

Now, the moral law makes us moral beings, which, in turn, makes us special: thanks to this we are "ends" and never simply "means," "persons" and not "things." From this, a new formulation of the moral law emerges (the "formula of humanity"): "Act in such a way that you treat humanity, whether in your own person or in the person of another, always at the same time as an end and never simply as a means."[7] So why are lying promises immoral again? Because, under this formulation, liars treat others simply as a means—as a means to a loan, in this particular example. In other words, liars disrespect others.

PROMOTE HAPPINESS! MILL'S VERSION OF THE MORAL LAW

Let us now turn to Mill's utilitarianism and switch the order of the questions (it is no coincidence that Mill himself presents the utilitarian principle before justifying it). So what does the moral law order? This is the closest one to get to a formulation: "The creed which accepts as the foundation of morals 'utility' or 'the greatest happiness principle' holds that actions are right in proportion as they tend to promote happiness; wrong as they tend to produce the reverse of happiness."[8]

It would have been nice if Mill had introduced the utilitarian principle as Kant does: neatly singled out and in the imperative form. Instead, Mill mixes it with a definition of utilitarianism and describes the criterion it contains to distinguish right from wrong. Kant, on the contrary, couches the moral law in opening words such as "Act as if . . ." and "Act in such a way. . . ." What would the utilitarian principle look like if we did the same? Something like this: "Act in such a way that you promote as much happiness and reduce as much unhappiness as possible in the world." Or, as it is popularly phrased: "Promote the greatest happiness for the greatest number of people."

Since the utilitarian principle would remain empty without a definition of that which we must promote—namely, happiness—Mill offers one: happiness is "pleasure and the absence of pain."[9] This definition of happiness allows us to make the utilitarian moral law even more precise: "Act in such a way that you promote as much pleasure and reduce as much pain as possible in the world." Or following the popular phrasing one more time: "Promote the greatest pleasure for the greatest number of people."

You may be wondering: Does Mill's definition of happiness as pleasure not make the theory vain and superfluous? Are we supposed to promote a world full of spas? No, unless corporeal pleasures are the only ones there are—which is not the case. Anticipating or responding to an actual critique, Mill takes the time to highlight the existence of what he calls "mental [noncorporeal] pleasures": "the pleasures of the intellect [e.g., reading Plato], of the feelings and imagination [e.g., listening to Leonard Cohen], and of the moral sentiments [e.g., spending a morning volunteering with friends]."[10] These pleasures, Mill further defends, are qualitatively higher than the corporeal, as those who know both recognize. According to this perspective, a world full of spas is not to be opposed, but given the choice between spas and libraries, we must opt for the libraries—higher happiness awaits there.

You may also be wondering: do we (each of us) have to calculate the consequences of everything we do to live a utilitarian life? Again, Mill says no. The calculation has, for the most part, been done throughout history by our predecessors: "During all that time mankind have been learning by experience the tendencies of actions."[11] This experience has taught us that there are certain things that hurt human happiness, and others that promote it. This is, in Mill's account, the origin of the same secondary duties that we find in Kant—principles that, together, constitute a basic moral code that all humans share (do not steal, do not lie, help the needy, and so on). So instead of becoming a refined utilitarian calculator, Mill invites us to rely on that basic moral code, confident that it is the best way to promote a less miserable world.

Note the further lesson from the last insight: utilitarianism does not allow the breaking of secondary duties like "do not lie" for the sake of general happiness, even if it looks like it does. Instead of choosing acts that promote general happiness in the short term for those directly affected, a utilitarian follows rules that promote general happiness in the long term and for society in general. Thus, I can be tempted, "for the purpose of getting

over some momentary embarrassment, or attaining some object immediately useful to ourselves or others, to tell a lie,"[12] but since lies hurt general
happiness in the long term and on a large scale, the utilitarian principle
commands telling the truth. There are exceptions, like lying to a murderer,
but these must be strongly justified.

TEXT BOX 1.2: JEREMY BENTHAM AND JOHN S. MILL

If Kant did not lead an exciting life (by ordinary standards), Mill certainly did—and so did his master, the founder of utilitarianism, Jeremy
Bentham.

Mill's intense life. Born in England in 1806, Mill had a very intense
father who taught him Greek and arithmetic at the age of 3, made him
read Plato at the age of 7, and asked him to edit his own books when
he was 11. When Mill turned 20, he suffered a mental breakdown from
which he luckily recovered.

At 24 he met Harriet Taylor, the love of his life. He had to wait 19
years to date her, though, since Taylor's husband decided to live a little
longer. They married two years after he finally died. Their marriage,
sadly, only lasted seven years, when Taylor herself passed away.

Mill not only published immensely influential books such as
Utilitarianism, On Liberty (1859), and *On the Subjection of Women* (1869),
but also participated in politics as a Member of Parliament. He died a
peaceful death in the company of his step-daughter, in 1873, after telling
her: "You know that I have done my work."[13]

Bentham's intense post-death. Born in England in 1748, Bentham was
also a prodigy. As Crisp records, "at age 3, on a visit to a country house,
he was bored by the conversation of his elders and retreated to the
library to carry out some historical research."[14] Like Mill, he was a philosopher and legal reformer, author of the groundbreaking *The Principles
of Morals and Legislation* (1789). He died in 1832.

The following anecdote, though, says of him more than a biography
of a thousand words could. In his will, Bentham requested that his
body be preserved as an auto-icon. His body has had an equally exciting life since then. At one point, for instance, his head was stolen (and
later recovered). His body even participated in a council meeting at the
University College London, where he rests today and where his writings
are currently being edited for publication. If you go to London, pay him
a visit—just don't take his head.

A CONSEQUENTIALIST COMMAND FROM
PLEASURE: THE MORAL LAW'S SOURCE IN MILL

It is tricky, in the case of Mill, to signal the source of the moral law. This may be due to his allegedly instrumental view of reason not as a legislator, but an instrument at the service of happiness—happiness that, as we saw, he identifies as pleasure. If this is so, the moral law must come from a place other than reason. But from where? For this, we must look at his proof of (his version of) the moral law.

This proof is highly controversial, but here it is:

1. Happiness (pleasure) is the only thing desired as an end.
∴ It is our primary duty to promote general happiness (pleasure).[15]

Like with any argument, this is the challenge: we must confirm that the premise is true and that the conclusion follows from it. And what is the case for it?

Let's start with the premise, to which Mill devotes most of his efforts. Is it true that the only thing we desire as an end is happiness (pleasure)?

Mill's strategy to prove the premise is to consider other candidates, i.e., other things people may desire as ends. Money, for instance. Money is a means to other things: from food to beach houses. Some people, though, desire it as an end in itself. They find pleasure in an increasingly beefy bank account. According to Mill, though, this would not prove the premise false because, as he argues:

> The ingredients of happiness [pleasure] are very various, and each of them is desirable in itself, and not merely when considered as swelling an aggregate. The principle of utility does not mean that any given pleasure, as music, for instance, or any given exemption from pain, as for example health, is to be looked upon as means to a collective something termed happiness. . . . They are desired and desirable in and for themselves; besides being means, they are a part of the end.[16]

The same goes for power, fame, and so forth. They are originally desired as means, but when they come to be desired as ends, as they can, they become the end, or part thereof, that is happiness (pleasure). As Mill insists, "happiness [pleasure] is not an abstract idea but a concrete whole; and these are some of its parts."[17] So yes, we can desire other things as ends, but when we do, they do not compete with happiness (pleasure)—this absorbs them.

The premise, you probably agree, is controversial. But if the premise is controversial, its connection with the conclusion is even more so. Assuming that happiness (pleasure) is the only thing each of us desires as an end, how could this give birth to an imperative to promote it for all? "I desire my happiness (pleasure). Therefore, I must promote everyone's happiness (pleasure)," the argument, or proof, goes. Mill says that the conclusion follows, "since a part [individual happiness (pleasure)] is included in the whole [general happiness (pleasure)],"[18] but not everyone sees the connection. Something seems missing. An additional premise, most probably.

Assuming that Mill does not succeed in proving the moral law (if this is indeed the case), this would not necessarily mean that utilitarianism is false, incidentally. It may instead mean that better proof is needed.

Now, back to our original question: What does this proof tell us about the source of the moral law? The best way I can express the answer is thus: according to the proof, the moral law is a normative insight from experience. If you recognize, as Mill thinks you should, that the only thing humans desire as an end is happiness (pleasure), then you must admit that it is your duty to promote as much happiness (pleasure) as possible in the world.

Another way to express its source is thus: if the highest good in life is happiness (pleasure), then the source of the moral law is happiness (pleasure). From this perspective, happiness (pleasure) commands itself: "I am the highest good; therefore, promote me," it says, and we should comply. Or so says Mill.

THE PATH TO A FREER WORLD: THE MORAL LAW'S IMPORTANCE IN KANT

As might be expected, Kant and Mill disagree on various points. They do not disagree on everything, though (more on that later). One of the ideas they both subscribe to is the moral law's importance. Here are four reasons why this is so according to Kant.

The first (and by now obvious) reason is that the moral law allows us to distinguish right from wrong. We judge the morality of our own and other's actions all the time, but how do we make these judgments? Or, as students are prone to ask, "Who says what is right and what is wrong?" Well, it is the moral law that springs from your own reason.

Kant argues that humans come into the world with a sort of moral software that lets them recognize if something is immoral (he does not use this precise analogy, of course, but you get the point). Every human, from the humblest to the most learned, has this ability. Thus, one does not to be a philosopher or enjoy "far-reaching acuteness"[19] to distinguish right from wrong—we are born with the moral law and the moral law awakens along with our reason.

Second, the moral law protects us from rationalization. Even though one does not have to be a moral philosopher to distinguish right from wrong, thinking about ethics and, more specifically, about the moral law that makes those judgments possible, protects us from our own deceptions.

Together with the power to distinguish right from wrong, humans have the power to rationalize—i.e., to justify—immoral behavior. Our needs and inclinations cloud our judgments, and a good way to protect us from this is "to take a step into the field of practical [moral] philosophy."[20] Why? Because good moral philosophy teaches us about the moral law. Now when we see the moral law face to face (as you have done in this chapter), we are better equipped to fight rationalization. How? By consciously resorting to the moral law every time we are tempted to do wrong.

Third, the moral law grounds human dignity—and basic rights. We spoke of the popularity of rights. But where do basic rights come from? Which is their moral source? The idea of basic rights cannot be just a convention, since conventions can change and we tend to think of basic rights as being intrinsic to human beings. Instead, basic rights come from human dignity. And where in turn does human dignity come from? It is to Kant that we are indebted for the best secular argument for human dignity and, by extension, for human rights (an argument preliminary advanced in the "formula of humanity" of the moral law). In short, humans have dignity since they are moral beings—beings, as we have seen, that are capable of distinguishing right from wrong thanks to the moral law that their own reason dictates. As Kant puts it: "Hence morality and humanity, insofar as it is capable of morality, alone have dignity."[21]

Fourth, the moral law is the path to autonomy or true freedom. All humans have dignity just by being humans. No matter how many terrible things someone does, the person does not become a thing, something with a price. But there is some higher status we can strive for: the aforementioned freedom. Again, we all have dignity, but only those who effectively place the moral law at the head of their decisions gain that extra sober yet exquisite reward. Freedom from what? From our needs and inclinations, from the objects of our desires. Instead of blindly obeying them, the will becomes "a law to itself."[22]

Think of the latter in this way. When I am hungry my desire for a hamburger claims authority over me. The desire pushes me toward the sandwich joint. Now, there is nothing wrong with feeding oneself, but let's say that, after getting the sandwich, I come across a starving child. Here something else happens: the moral law activates itself, ordering me to share my food. Suddenly I have two choices: obey my hunger or obey the moral law. If I share it, I would have overcomed the law of hunger by affirming my own (but universal) law.

TEXT BOX 1.3. KANT ON HAPPINESS AND RELATED TOPICS

The role of happiness in ethics is very different in Kant and in Mill. For Kant, happiness is important, but secondary. But what does Kant say about happiness?

Can happiness ground ethics? For Kant, ethics is not primarily about what makes us happy, but about being good. As he contends, "this principle [of happiness] contributes nothing to the establishment of morality, inasmuch as making a man happy is quite different from making him good and making him prudent and sharp-sighted for his own advantage quite different from making him virtuous."[23]

What is happiness? Kant does not define happiness except as the satisfaction of our needs and inclinations. On this basis, it is not possible to offer a conclusive recipe for a happy life. Happiness has a chameleonic nature: one "can never say definitively and consistently what it is that he really wishes and wills."[24] Another reason to ground ethics in another place.

Does not the moral law make us happy? The moral law often requires that we renounce happiness. Still, one can say that doing the right thing feels good. So what is going on? Kant recognizes this feeling in another book and names it "contentment with oneself."[25] But contentment, the feeling that comes with doing the right thing, is not happiness—which, again, is the satisfaction of our needs and inclinations.

Can we hope for happiness? Let's say I live an ethical life but misfortune hits me again and again. I am content, but miserable. Can I hope for happiness? Yes. For Kant it is reasonable to expect that if you are ethical (if you follow the categorical imperative), you will be rewarded in a future life. This Kant calls the highest good, which is "God's final end in creating the world."[26]

Happiness, then, has a place in Kant's ethics.[27] In fact, he would not be a great moral philosopher if he simply rejected it—which, as explained, he simply does not.

THE PATH TO A HAPPIER WORLD:
THE MORAL LAW'S IMPORTANCE IN MILL

In Mill as well the moral law allows right to be distinguished from wrong. There is nothing to say about this first reason for the importance of the moral law that was not said in the previous section—except that, for Mill, this law does not spring from reason.

Do you want to do something but you are not sure if it is ethical? If after consulting the rules of humanity's moral code you are still genuinely doubtful, go on and ponder whether the world will be a better place following your action. But do not forget: think long term and on a big scale. Breaking a moral duty like "do not lie" (or any other) should only happen in extreme cases and be duly justified by the moral law. Suspect your motivation for breaking the duty—most probably you are just trying to serve yourself.

Second, the moral law is the path to a happier world. If humans followed it, a lot of suffering would vanish. People would be much more concerned about promoting happiness and reducing suffering in the world—in accordance with their means, of course. It is no coincidence that one of the most influential altruistic movements of our time, "effective altruism," was created and is being led by the most influential utilitarian alive, Peter Singer. As the movement's eponymous website says, effective altruism answers one question:

> How can we use our resources to help others the most? Rather than just doing what feels right, we use evidence and careful analysis to find the very best causes to work on. But it's no use answering the question unless you act on it. Effective altruism is about following through. It's about being generous with your time and your money to do the most good you can.[28]

With books and websites such as "The Life You Can Save,"[29] "Doing Good Better,"[30] and "Give Well,"[31] this utilitarian-inspired movement is indeed striving to reduce suffering in the world. And not just for humans, but for animals as well.[32]

Third, the moral law grounds basic rights. Just like Kant's ethics, utilitarianism offers a ground for the defense of fundamental, individual rights. In Mill, though, this does not happen through the concept of human dignity, but through the moral law itself. There are no intermediaries.

Think, for instance, of freedom of speech. It is a right, right? It is insofar as societies that enjoy it are happier than those that don't. There are several explanations for why this is the case. One obvious reason is the advancement of knowledge. Just imagine if every official "truth" in history was never questioned. One thing is sure: I would not be writing a book *on* ethics *with* a laptop—and you would not be reading it.

By grounding basic rights in the moral law, Mill offers us a way to solve controversial issues like, say, abortion and gender identity. Do you want to know if they (and animal rights, universal basic income, etcetera) are indeed rights? Ponder whether the world would be happier with them. Note that Mill himself pondered rights that were not recognized in his times, like the right to equal treatment between men and women.[33]

Note further that if at the individual level we are not supposed to calculate the consequences of everything we do, in the public sphere the calculus seems fundamental. Of course, we do not need to do a utilitarian calculus to ban digital theft, but we may need one to evaluate whether we should establish the death penalty.[34] In fact, Mill is convinced that polarization in politics would be substantially reduced if utilitarianism reigned.

To some, grounding basic rights in the utilitarian principle leaves rights vulnerable. But this (like other topics outlined here) is material for another book.

KANT AND MILL: CHAMPIONS OF THE MORAL LAW

It is natural, when studying Kant's and Mill's ethics, to focus on the things that divide them. The basic differences are obvious. For Kant, the source of the moral law is reason; for Mill, pleasure. For Mill, actions are right in accordance with their consequences; for Kant, they are right in themselves. For Kant, the moral law orders to act in accordance with maxims that one can will become universal laws; for Mill, to promote the greatest amount of happiness for the greatest amount of people. Etcetera.

There are, though, substantial agreements that are rarely highlighted. This can have a negative impact on advocates of ethics: instead of leaving the topic (approached through a class or a book) with a clearer idea of what ethics is, in essence, about, students end up more confused than when they arrived: "If not even the great moral thinkers of all time can agree on their object of study, there must be nothing to agree about and ethics must therefore be totally subjective." So here are some of the things they agree upon. A few of them are obvious, but they are so obvious that we may miss them (just as we miss things that are too close to us).

Let's begin by saying that both Kant and Mill believe that ethics is objective. They would be appalled by the moral relativism that has gained traction since the twentieth century. I imagine them wondering: "Are moral relativists coherent enough to regard the radical immorality of murdering innocents as something debatable?" They would be more appalled to realize that this position flourished right after the Holocaust. Mill and Kant, conversely, were convinced of the reality of objective, some even obvious, moral truths.

Not only were Kant and Mill moral objectivists, but both also believed that such objectivity was rooted in a supreme principle: the moral law. They both speak of it, defend it, and believe it to be the source of other fundamental moral realities—the secondary duties of morality and basic rights, to begin with.

With regard to the secondary duties of morality, in the *Grounding* Kant works out the duties of not committing suicide, keeping one's promises, developing our talents, helping those in need, and so on. In *Utilitarianism*, we find Mill speaking of the duties of not killing, not stealing, not lying, etcetera. Granted, they do not mention the exact same set of duties in these specific works, but their lists are not exhaustive and there is every indication that they would agree on most, if not all, the duties contained in each other's lists.

Think of suicide. Would Mill not also condemn it? Surprisingly, he never takes a clear position on the ethics of suicide,[35] but there are reasons to think he would regard it immoral. To begin with, "do not commit suicide" belongs to those rules of tradition that Mill backs up—rules that, he argues, are the result of a sort of historical utilitarian calculus. And even if we doubt whether the rule serves general happiness, it would not be hard to demonstrate that suicide leaves the world worse off—traumatized spouses, parents, sons and daughters, friends—in addition to setting a bad example for society.

Now, regarding basic rights, we have seen how both philosophers argue that the moral law grounds them. As in everything else, they have different reasons for this, but on whether there are basic rights grounded in the moral law, they shake hands. In Kant, basic rights spring from dignity, dignity that in turn springs from the moral law within us. In Mill, basic rights are instead grounded in the duty to promote general happiness: we must protect basic rights such as freedom of thought and expression because the world is happier when we protect them—and we must promote happiness. The rights that both espouse, though, are the typical rights of a modern liberal society: life, property, liberty of thought, and so forth.

These agreements are not trivial and they strengthen the thesis that ethics is objective. (In addition, these agreements will later allow us to summon both thinkers for our analysis of why conflicts of interest are morally problematic.)

TEXT BOX 1.4: MILL ON FREEDOM

If Kant's ethics is about freedom or autonomy, Mill's is about happiness. But what does Mill say about freedom? For that, we must read *On Liberty*.

A book on political philosophy. The book is not about ethics but about political philosophy. Its goal is to set "the nature and limits of the power which can be legitimately exercised by society over the individual."[36] It is a book that aims at defending people's civil liberty—and rights. But what is said limit? And why will someone concerned with general happiness want to limit a government's power?

The harm principle. The limit is the following: "The only purpose for which power can be rightfully exercised over any member of a civilised community, against his will, is to prevent harm to others."[37] If the action does not harm others, society should not intervene. This is known as the (rather liberal) harm principle. But why? What justifies the harm principle? You guessed it: the utilitarian principle.

The justification. Societies should not limit people's liberty because of dignity in the Kantian, i.e., the metaphysical, sense, but because those that do so are happier. In other words, the most efficient way to promote the greatest amount of happiness for the greatest amount of people is to secure liberty. Liberty or freedom is a means to general happiness. "I regard utility as the ultimate appeal on all ethical questions."[38]

An example: liberty of thought and discussion. Why should societies protect this? For the sake of general happiness: (1) The censured opinion may be the truth; (2) Even if the censured opinion is false, "it may . . . contain a portion of truth";[39] (3) Even if the official opinion is entirely true, it can be professed as a prejudice; (4) Assuming again that the official opinion is entirely true, it could lose its force over our conduct.

This applies not only to liberty of thought and discussion. Any controversial right or topic can be solved through the utilitarian principle, according to Mill.

KANT AND MILL ON THE ESSENCE OF MORAL PROBLEMS

This is an additional agreement that deserves its own section: both Kant and Mill see ethics as a struggle between the moral law and our needs and inclinations.

In Kant, this is pretty clear. We can (re)confirm this very easily, by looking at those sections in which he derives some secondary moral duties from the moral law. There he presents the cases of "a man reduced to despair by a series of misfortunes [who, because of this] feels sick of life"[40] and who, in turn, considers suicide; of "another man in need [who] finds himself forced to borrow money" and who "knows very well that he won't be able to repay it";[41] of "a third [person who] finds in himself a talent whose cultivation could make him a man useful in many respects" but who "finds himself in comfortable circumstances and prefers to indulge in pleasure";[42] and of "a fourth man [who] finds things going well for himself but sees others (whom he could help) struggling with greater hardships" and who thinks "what does it matter to me?"[43] All these individuals, though, confront the moral law (the categorical imperative) and discover that it would be immoral to do what they are inclined to do. As Kant explains in another section:

> Man feels within himself a powerful counterweight to all the commands of duty, which are presented to him by reason as being so pre-eminently worthy of respect; this counterweight consists of his needs and inclinations, whose total satisfaction is summed up under the name of happiness.[44]

Two independent forces, then, seem to operate within us, many times pulling us in different directions, fighting to rule our lives: our desire for happiness and the moral law. In this light, a moral problem is a situation in which a need or inclination (an interest) tempts us to break a moral duty. True wisdom, in turn, consists in giving the moral law the priority it deserves (considering its pure source and its categorical nature).

Is this also the case in Mill? Yes. This is why utilitarianism is not a theory that purports moral egoism. As Mill himself says to those who think it is:

> the happiness which forms the utilitarian standard of what is right and wrong in conduct is not the agent's own happiness but that of all concerned. As between his own happiness and that of others, utilitarianism requires him to be as strictly impartial as a *disinterested* [emphasis added] and benevolent spectator.[45]

Utilitarian ethics, then, will sometimes demand the sacrifice of our happiness for that of others. In other words, the moral law (the utilitarian principle) is not always in harmony with our desires. Just like with Kant, for Mill they are independent forces that sometimes pull us in opposite directions. But this is why being ethical is hard, right? If this is indeed the case, Mill will define moral problems in the same way: as situations in which an interest tempts us to disregard a moral duty.

The ideal for Mill, of course, is to approach a stage in which individuals see

> an indissoluble association between his own happiness and the good of the whole, especially between his own happiness and the practice of such modes of conduct, negative and positive, as regard for the universal happiness prescribes; so that not only he may be unable to conceive the possibility of happiness to himself consistently with conduct opposed to the general good, but also that a direct impulse to promote the general good may be in every individual one of the habitual motives of action, and the sentiments connected therewith may fill a large and prominent place in every human being's sentient existence.[46]

But this is an ideal. Most of us, instead, do feel a tension between our own desire for happiness and the moral law. And until we dissolve this tension, moral problems will continue to exist (just like they exist in the Kantian view of ethics).

CHAPTER SUMMARY

This introductory chapter on ethics discussed the origin, formulation, and importance of the moral law—beginning with Kant's deontology. With regard to the first, we outlined Kant's thesis of the moral law as a categorical imperative that springs from our own reason (as distinguished from hypothetical imperatives).

With regard to the second, the chapter introduced two ways of formulating the moral law or categorical imperative in the Kantian version: the formula of universal law and the formula of humanity. In the formula of universal law, the moral law orders to "Act only according to that maxim whereby you can, at the same time, will that it should become a universal law." In the formula of humanity, in turn, the moral law orders to "Act in such a way that you treat humanity, whether in your own person or in the person of another, always at the same time as an end and never simply as a means."

The chapter then turned to Mill's utilitarianism, and more specifically to the formulation of the moral law: "Promote the greatest happiness for the greatest number of people." And what is happiness, according to this theory? Pleasure and the absence of pain. The pleasure that we must promote, let's remember, is not only corporeal but mental or spiritual as well.

After presenting the formulation of the principle of utility, the chapter discussed its potential origin. More specifically, it discussed Mill's proof of the principle: if it is true, as he thinks, that happiness (pleasure) is the only thing desired as an end, then the principle of utility follows. But is the premise true? And does the conclusion really follow from it? The question, as almost everything in philosophy, remains open.

The chapter then discussed the importance of the moral law according to Kant: it allows us to distinguish right from wrong, shields us against rationalization, grounds human dignity (and thus human rights), and is the path to autonomy or true freedom. Some of the reasons for the importance of the moral law according to Mill are the same, but not all coincide: for Mill, besides allowing us to distinguish right from wrong, the moral law is the path to a happier world, and grounds basic rights (although not through human dignity).

The chapter then identified things in common between Kant's deontology and Mill's utilitarianism. First, both believe that ethics is objective. Second, both believe that such objectivity is grounded in the moral law. Third, both believe that the moral law is the source of more concrete, secondary moral duties. Fourth, both believe that the moral law grounds basic rights. Fifth and finally, both see moral problems in the same way: as situations in which an interest tempts us to disregard the moral law and the duties it begets.

Then, parallel sections presented biographical information about Kant and Mill (as well as Bentham) and discussed Kant's view of happiness and Mill's view of freedom.

Some readers may be wondering, how are these theories part of the "spirit of our times," as suggested in this chapter's introduction? Kant's categorical imperative, and his ethics in general, is alive in the almost universal present-day belief in human rights. But how so, if he was primarily interested in duties? Again, through his argument for dignity: we have dignity because we are moral beings, and we are moral beings thanks to the moral law.

Mill's principle of utility, in turn, is alive in another widely shared belief: the importance of the consequences of what we do on human suffering. Bentham and Mill were not the first to consider this, of course, but they did put consequences and human suffering under the spotlight. So every time we rely on the consequences of anything to judge it, we are in a way summoning the utilitarian principle.

To the extent that we still believe in human rights and care about consequences and suffering, we are, in a way, both Kantians and utilitarians.

QUESTIONS AND EXERCISES FOR REFLECTION

1. Before reading this chapter, had you ever heard of the moral law?
2. What is the moral law, according to Kant? And where does it come from?
3. What is the moral law, according to Mill? And where does it come from?
4. What does the moral law order, according to Kant?
5. What does the moral law order, according to Mill?
6. Why is the moral law important to ethics, according to Kant?
7. Why is the moral law important to ethics, according to Mill?
8. Imagine that Kant and Mill go to a bar to discuss ethics. Do you think they could reach an agreement regarding it, or do they disagree on everything? Explain.
9. What is the essence or basic structure of moral problems?
10. Can we coherently integrate Kant's and Mill's ethics? Explain.
11. After reading this chapter, do you think ethics is objective? Why? Include the moral law in your analysis.
12. Why do you think the moral law has almost disappeared from public discourse? Or do you think it is still present?

Chapter 2

BUSINESS ETHICS AND CORPORATE SOCIAL RESPONSIBILITY

"The term 'being' is used in many senses," says Aristotle in the *Metaphysics*.[1]

Inspired by his insight, we might also note that the term "business ethics" is used in many senses as well. And what is the most common way in which business ethics is used? Corporate Social Responsibility.

You will have heard of it. Corporate social responsibility is a management theory that advocates, among other things, the consideration in all business decisions of the dignity and interests of all parties who may be affected by a business: employees, suppliers, etcetera. In other words, it champions a way of doing business that responds to the demands of society—that takes responsibility for how business activities affect society. (Thus, it not only encompasses environmentalism but transcends it).

Perhaps, the most popular version of corporate social responsibility is R. Edward Freeman's *stakeholder theory*—as presented, for instance, in "Managing for Stakeholders." Freeman's proposition emerged in the mid-1970s as a reaction to a preexisting view that placed shareholders as the top priority.

Corporate social responsibility, though, must be older, since Milton Friedman was already attacking it in the 1960s. Specifically, in *Capitalism and Freedom* (1962), Friedman argued that the concept undermines capitalism and, as a consequence, freedom. Later, in 1970, Friedman published a short piece in the *New York Times Magazine*, "The Social Responsibility of Business is to Increase its Profits," that served as a sort of pamphlet for his alternative *shareholder theory*.

So which came first? Let's just say that shareholder theory is older than corporate social responsibility; that, as noted, Friedman decided to attack the latter when it arose; and that, after this attack, Freeman resolved to leap to its defense with his stakeholder theory. But there are more pressing questions, like whether corporate social responsibility is well-grounded and how it relates to conflicts of interest.

In this chapter, I deal with these questions. I start with an outline of Friedman's shareholder theory and, in particular, of his *moral argument* against corporate social responsibility. I then introduce Freeman's stakeholder theory—his *descriptive* and *normative arguments*—against the shareholder theory, as well as the grounds for the duty of executives to care for the interests of all stakeholders. I will then return to Friedman's shareholder theory and explain how, despite Freeman's arguments against it, it still stands, housing a good number of businesspeople (and some researchers).

After introducing and comparing the stakeholder and the shareholder theories, I link both theories with conflicts of interest. We will see how, despite not dealing with conflicts of interest expressly, there are elements in both that allow us to speculate about their (very different) stances on the topic.

I will close this chapter by presenting a critique that can be leveled at both the stakeholder theory and the shareholder theory: the *problem of elitism*, in that both address business executives rather than all employees. This, in turn, will make the case for a greater attention to be paid to conflicts of interest in the business ethics debate. Why? Because conflicts of interest, unlike corporate social responsibility problems, affect all employees, not only those at the top—as we will see.

My foremost intention in writing this chapter is to move readers from their probable current stance—the corporate social responsibility approach to business ethics—to consider conflicts of interest. In so doing, we will have moved from ethics to corporate social responsibility, and from corporate social responsibility to conflicts of interest.

SHAREHOLDER THEORY 1: THE CASE AGAINST CORPORATE SOCIAL RESPONSIBILITY

Friedman is a fierce critic of corporate social responsibility. Because of this, he is often thought of as the enemy of ethics in business—that is, as someone who might justify anything a company does in the name of profits. We will soon see whether this portrait is fair.

In "The Social Responsibility of Business is to Increase its Profits," Friedman presents a *political argument* against corporate social responsibility. In short, he thinks that businesspeople that promote it are, unconsciously, eroding the foundations of free markets and, as a consequence, of free societies. Considering exactly why he thinks this is the case is the burden of his article.

We are not here, though, to do politics but to consider ethics. The fact is that we can extract a purely moral argument against corporate social responsibility from Friedman's text. This moral argument begins with a preliminary point: when debating corporate social responsibility, we should first identify those who are called to implement it. So who are they? Business executives (hence, Friedman's essay could also have been titled "The Social Responsibility of *Business Executives* is to Increase *the Company's Profits*").

What is the core responsibility of business executives? As employees of the business owners, their responsibility is nothing other than "to conduct the business in accordance with their desires [and interests, we might also say], which generally will be to make as much money as possible."[2]

This idea of executives being at the service of shareholders' interests may strike one as extreme, but think of your own case when you hire someone. Don't you hire a person to do something you want—something like fixing your car, or cutting your hair?

> The problem with "socially responsible" business executives would be that, instead of fulfilling their contractual responsibility, they take the liberty to pursue a different agenda. More concretely, instead of reproducing shareholders' money, which is their freely assumed job, business executives who embrace corporate social responsibility take part of that money and use it for different ends.[3]

This, Friedman says, is immoral, based on the following argument:

1. The responsibility of business executives is to fulfill shareholders' interests.
2. The interests of shareholders lie (ordinarily) in making as much money as possible.
3. Corporate social responsibility policies reduce shareholders' profits.
4. By promoting corporate social responsibility, business executives betray their main responsibility.
5. Betraying a freely taken responsibility is immoral.
∴ Executives who promote corporate social responsibility policies act immorally.

Of all these premises, corporate social responsibility enthusiasts tend to focus on the third and attempt to show that it is false. Consider the benefits that Philip Kotler and Nancy Lee associate with corporate social responsibility: (a) increased sales and market share, (b) strengthened brand positioning, (c) enhanced corporate image and clout, (d) increased ability to attract, motivate, and retain employees, (e) decreased operational costs, and (f) increased appeal to investors and financial analysts.[4]

If the case for the profitability of corporate social responsibility were closed, then not only the third premise but also the fourth would turn out to be false. On this basis, the whole argument against it would fall apart. Indeed, the conclusion would be the opposite: business executives who promote corporate social responsibility act morally, since this is a path to profits.

Corporate social responsibility policies, though, can be expensive to the point where they outweigh the benefits, thereby reducing shareholders' returns. This prompts quantitative questions with regard to the amount of money companies should invest in corporate social responsibility to ensure its profitability, the very possibility of quantifying its benefits, and so on. The fourth premise of Friedman's argument, then, cannot be dismissed so easily.

TEXT BOX 2.1: "SOCIALLY RESPONSIBLE" SHAREHOLDERS AND INDIVIDUAL PROPRIETORS

Friedman's discussion of corporate social responsibility focuses primarily on executives, but he also has some words for "socially responsible" shareholders and individual proprietors.

To begin with, he thinks that the same (political and moral) arguments apply to the case of shareholders. Corporations have several shareholders and some of them can be expected to promote corporate social responsibility, pushing other shareholders to do likewise. Friedman is not impressed by them:

> In most of these cases, what is in effect involved is some stockholders trying to get other stockholders . . . to contribute *against their will* [emphasis added] to "social" causes favoured by the activists. Insofar as they succeed, they are again imposing taxes and spending the proceeds.[5]

When it comes to individual proprietors, the case is different and more simple: the company's money is their money, so they can do whatever they want, including being as "socially responsible" as they want:

> If he [the individual proprietor] acts to reduce the returns of his enterprise in order to exercise his "social responsibility," he is spending his own money, not someone else's. If he wishes to spend his money on such purposes, that is his right, and I cannot see that there is any objection to his doing so.[6]

But Friedman might have seen a problem here as well. If his political argument against corporate social responsibility is right, then not even individual proprietors should embrace it. Why? Because they would be undermining free markets and free societies.

Take the case of Dan Price, owner of Gravity Payments, who in 2015 became famous for reducing his salary from US$1,000,000 to US$70,000 to raise the salary of his employees.[7] This prompted calls to increase the minimum wage. Price was later seen (in 2020) advocating a new payroll tax to support housing for the homeless.[8]

STAKEHOLDER THEORY 1: A CRITIQUE OF THE SHAREHOLDER THEORY

Defenders of corporate social responsibility do not give up easily, and the boldest among them have developed a whole theory around it: stakeholder theory, which begins with a critique of Friedman's shareholder theory.

In "Managing for Stakeholders," Freeman presents two arguments against shareholder theory, which, as we have seen, puts owners' desires above the interests of others: that it is inconsistent with the law (the descriptive argument) and with ethics (the normative argument).

In his descriptive argument, Freeman contends that shareholder theory is inconsistent with the law, which has evolved to demand that businesses (and business executives) consider the interests of any party—that is, any stakeholder, whether customers, employees, communities, or others—that might be adversely affected by their activities.

In the case of customers, for instance, the old *caveat emptor* has been replaced with *caveat venditor*, i.e., with the principle that sellers, and not buyers, are responsible for what is sold (based on cases such as *Greenman v. Yuba Power*).[9] Employees also have more rights now than they had, say, a hundred years ago—through laws such as the National Labor Relations

Act (1935),[10] the Age Discrimination Act (1967),[11] and others. The same phenomenon can be seen in environmental law, which benefits communities, and so on.

This argument would be restricted to the United States if that country's tendency to regulate the responsibility of business to stakeholders were an exception—but the tendency is global (if you are not from the United States, think of your own country's law).[12] Companies therefore cannot increase, with impunity, owners' profits at the expense of the interests of other stakeholders. The shareholder theory, thus, "is simply a myth"[13] that does not adequately describe how businesses operate today (hence the descriptive nature of the argument).

Moving to the normative argument, which holds that shareholder theory is also inconsistent with ethics. In other words, from a normative perspective, and regardless of what the law says, businesses should consider, in their activities, the interests of all stakeholders and not just those of their shareholders.

Here, Freeman presents the *separation fallacy*, the *open question argument*, the *integration thesis*, and the *responsibility principle*. Together, he proposes, they debunk the shareholder theory and prepare the ground for his stakeholder theory.

The separation fallacy is the mistaken idea that business decisions should not be mixed with ethics—i.e., that it is better to keep both realms apart. This is a fallacy that, according to Freeman, the shareholder theory embraces.

Through the open question argument, Freeman wants us to begin seeing why the separation thesis is fallacious. More specifically, he asks us if, faced with any business decision, ethical questions like "who does this decision harm and/or benefit?" fit into the deliberative process. Since ethical questions do in fact fit into the process, the idea that business decisions are independent of ethics proves to be false.

While exposing the separation thesis as fallacious, the open question argument opens the door to the integration thesis, which holds that "most business decisions . . . have some ethical content or implicit ethical view."[14]

Finally, with the responsibility principle, Freeman finds common ground between different ethical views—ground that will lead to a different, ethical view of business in the form of the stakeholder theory. This principle proposes that "most people, most of the time, want to, actually do, and should accept responsibility for the effects of their actions on others."[15] In this text, Freeman does not prove that people regularly want and do accept responsibility. He instead focuses on the "should" element of the statement.

STAKEHOLDER THEORY 2: MANAGING
FOR STAKEHOLDERS

The arguments against shareholder theory can be outlined as follows:

1. Shareholder theory holds that the responsibility of businesses and business executives is to increase shareholders' profits.
2. Through law, businesses have evolved to consider all stakeholders' interests.
3. Under the responsibility principle, businesses and business executives have a moral responsibility to consider stakeholders' interests.

∴ The shareholder theory is both unreal and unethical.

But what does the stakeholder theory actually propose? It proposes a *new vision of business* and specifies the (purportedly) *true responsibility of business executives*.

Let's begin with the new vision of business. Freeman sees the business world interacting with people who have joint interests to fulfill these interests while creating value. That those interests are common becomes clear when we consider questions like these:

> How could a bondholder recognize any returns without management paying attention to the stakes of costumers or employees? How could costumers get the products and services they need without employees and suppliers? How could employees have a decent place to live without communities.[16]

Freeman does not deny that the interests, despite being joint, many sometimes give rise to conflict. He challenges us, though, to focus on their interdependence and work toward their satisfaction. And, in fact, why not do that whenever possible? Why not try to harmonize and fulfill all stakeholders' interests, converting problems into win–win–win–(etcetera) situations?

The true responsibility of business executives, for its part, is "to create as much values as possible for [all] stakeholders."[17] This is another way to put the last idea—one that Freeman further backs up with four philosophical arguments. We will focus on the first two—to the extent that they correspond to the moral theories we reviewed earlier and to the extent that they suffice to ground Freeman's point.

The first argument is the *argument from consequences* (which corresponds, broadly speaking, to Mill's utilitarianism). Here, Freeman contests the doctrine of the "invisible hand,"[18] according to which selfishness promotes the best consequences for society. But does the opposite not make more sense? Would we not all be better off if we cooperated, provided we see ourselves as friends rather than as enemies? If this is the case (as common sense suggests) and if it is a moral duty (as consequentialists defend) to make decisions that leave the world better off, then embracing it would be a moral duty. In other words, it would be a moral duty for executives to shun selfishness and consider the interests of all other stakeholders in every business decision they make.

The second argument is the *argument from rights* (which corresponds to Kant's deontology). Remember how, according to Kant, the moral law from reason confers upon humans a special status: dignity. And remember how dignity is the source of human rights. Well, if it is the case that humans have intrinsic rights, then these rights must be honored. Otherwise, we would be using humans merely as means. In the business world, this means that businesspeople should honor the dignity and rights of the stakeholders. Freeman expresses his point as follows: "But, if executives take managing for stakeholders seriously, they will automatically think about what is owed to customers, suppliers, employees, financiers, and communities, in virtue of their stake, and in virtue of their basic humanity."[19]

TEXT BOX 2.2: FREEMAN'S ADDITIONAL ARGUMENTS

Besides the consequentialist and the deontological analysis, Freeman offers two more arguments for stakeholder theory: an *argument from character* and a *pragmatic argument*.

The argument from character is rooted in virtue ethics—the ethics of Socrates, Plato, and Aristotle. This theory holds that there is a human function, which is to reason, and that the good life means exercising that function virtuously. Freeman does not unfold these details, or even clarify whether he agrees with them (or if he instead sides with a contemporary, non-metaphysical virtue ethics). He simply says that if virtues play a role in a good life, then stakeholder theory is the way to go. Now, under shareholder theory, the only virtue that matters is loyalty to shareholders. Stakeholder theory, on the contrary, encourages several other virtues: "efficiency, fairness, respect, integrity, keeping commitments, and others are critical in being successful at creating value for stakeholders."[20]

The pragmatic argument, in turn, is rooted in, well, pragmatism—the philosophy of William James, John Dewey, and Richard Rorty. As Gregory Pence defines it in *A Dictionary of Common Philosophical Terms*, pragmatism "holds the truth of an idea should be measured by its practical application in the ordinary world."[21] Freeman further explains that "pragmatists want to know how we can live better, how we can create both ourselves and our communities in ways where values such as freedom and solidarity are present in our everyday lives to maximal extent."[22] The stakeholder theory will apparently match the pragmatic attitude. Not only that, but it would also work in practice, i.e., it would effectively lead to a better state of affairs. The pragmatist's argument will, in this way, complete the other ones, closing the case in favor of stakeholder theory.

SHAREHOLDER THEORY 2: THE LIMITS OF SHAREHOLDERS' DESIRES

Some pages ago I quoted Friedman's thoughts about the main responsibility of business executives. I did not present his complete characterization, though, and I did not on purpose. To what end? To show you the impression that people who have not read Friedman have of him—that of a man for whom business executives are merely uncritical servants of unscrupulous, greedy owners. These are his complete words:

> That responsibility is to conduct the business in accordance with their desires, which generally will be to make as much money as possible *while conforming to the basic rules of the society, both those embodied in law and those embodied I ethical custom* [emphasis added].[23]

Well, this changes things a little bit, doesn't it? Specifically, it changes the first premise of Friedman's moral argument against the stakeholder theory and further clarifies that he is not the arch-enemy of ethics in business after all:

1. The responsibility of business executives is to fulfill shareholders' interests *in a legal and ethical way*.
2. The interests of shareholders lie (ordinarily) in making as much money as possible.
3. Corporate social responsibility policies *go beyond law and ethics and* reduce shareholders' profits.
4. By promoting corporate social responsibility, business executives betray their main responsibility.
5. Betraying a freely taken responsibility is immoral.

∴. Executives who promote corporate social responsibility policies act immorally.

What this means in practice is that, in their efforts to reproduce shareholder's money, which is their responsibility as employees, business executives should not break higher responsibilities, which are those of law and ethics. They should not, for instance, increase the company's profits by lying to their clients or exploiting workers.

You may be thinking: "This is exactly what corporate social responsibility is about—to do business responsibly, i.e., legally and ethically!" Friedman does not see it this way. Rather, he apparently sees law and ethics as establishing moral minimums, and corporate social responsibility as demanding more—and arbitrarily so.

Think of the following list of corporate social initiatives a business executive can adopt, according to Kotler and Lee: (a) corporate cause promotions, (b) cause-related marketing, (c) corporate social marketing, (d) corporate philanthropy, (e) community volunteering, and (f) socially responsible business practices.[24] Now consider corporate philanthropy. Let's say that a socially responsible business executive decides to donate 5 percent of the company's yearly income to Greenpeace. Would she not be going beyond what the law and basic ethical standards demand? If the company operates in a serious country and is paying taxes and complying with environmental laws, it might very well be argued that she is. The fact is that the duty of charity cannot be extended to artificial persons like corporations.[25] Business executives have that duty but as human beings, not as agents of their employers.

The only way, in Friedman's view, that a business executive could justify such a donation without breaking the freely assumed responsibility of maximizing shareholders' money, is by proving that it would bring high returns—a very difficult task.

Friedman's article is still relevant and controversial. This is partly due to its "politically incorrect" political argument that corporate social responsibility leads to totalitarian socialism. It is also due, though, to the strength of his moral argument.

REVISITING FREEMAN'S CRITIQUE: DEBATING WITH A STRAW MAN?

Let's recall Freeman's argument against shareholder theory:

1. Shareholder theory holds that the responsibility of businesses and business executives is to increase shareholders' profits.

2. Through law, businesses have evolved to consider all stakeholders' interests.
3. Under the responsibility principle, businesses and business executives have a moral responsibility to consider stakeholders' interests.
∴ The shareholder theory is both unreal and unethical.

The problem with this argument is that, as we have just seen, Friedman's shareholder theory does recognize the place of law and ethics in business decisions. The second and third premises of Freeman's critique, then, would not correspond to reality—and thus the whole argument seems to fall apart.

This unraveling can prompt at least two reactions. The first is excitement on the part of shareholder theory enthusiasts. "Stakeholder theory," they would say, "is built on a weak critique of shareholder theory. If the critique crumbles, then stakeholder theory crumbles as well." "And also," they would continue, "Friedman was right all along! The main responsibility of business executives is to maximise shareholders' profits (within, of course, the limits of law and ethics)."

Another reaction is the following. Stakeholder theory is right but so is shareholder theory. Ultimately, both endorse the ethical management of businesses. Both would condemn Volkswagen's "dieselgate," Enron's fraud, Maddof's Ponzi scheme, and other such dubious practices. The debate is less complex than it seems—a misreading perhaps ignited by Friedman's combative style and by a superficial reading of his work.

There is a grain of truth in this interpretation. Freeman himself recognizes Friedman's general commitment to law and ethics.[26] It is Friedman's exponents and, I would add, his critics who present an incomplete view of his shareholder theory. It is they who are playing with a straw man. In my case, and perhaps in yours as well, it was not until I actually read him that I realized Friedman was not advocating unscrupulous businesses.

Shareholder theory and stakeholder theory, then, are more closely related than we tend to think, but can they be equated? If we judge the theories by their names, and their stand on corporate social responsibility, the answer is no. The first holds that shareholders' interests have primacy; the second, that all stakeholders' interests weigh the same. The first criticizes corporate social responsibility; the second champions it. What is going on?

I think the difference is this. Freeman argues persuasively that business executives should consider the dignity, and thus the interests, of all stakeholders when making a decision. But, as we have seen, he then equates this with a duty to "create as much value as possible for stakeholders."[27] Is this equivalence correct or is the formulation of executives' responsibility more demanding? I think the latter is the case.

Remember what we noted a few pages ago: "It seems he [Friedman] sees law and ethics as establishing moral minimums, and corporate social responsibility as demanding much more—and arbitrarily so." Remember as well how we reasoned that this can be true: some corporate social initiatives are too demanding. If this is so, then although Friedman and Freeman would agree about the moral need to respect stakeholders' humanity and interests when making a business decision, Friedman would protest the notion of going beyond this sober but legal and ethical stance. In other words, Friedman would warn us not to get carried away with corporate social responsibility. He would condemn, for instance, volunteering programs that take place during working hours. Why should we not get carried away again? Because when we do, we use others' resources for unauthorized purposes.

TEXT BOX 2.3: STAKEHOLDERS' STAKES

Speaking of stakeholders, who are they and what do they ordinarily want? To visualize them, Freeman offers an image of a circle surrounded by two rings.[28] The circle represents the corporation, the inner ring the primary stakeholders, and the outer ring the secondary stakeholders.

Before going on to list stakeholders and their interests, one might expect a definition of "stakeholder." Freeman gathers together several and rejects, for pragmatic purposes, the need to stick with one. From the definitions he cites, we can conclude that a stakeholder is an individual or group that can affect or be affected by the company, and that makes the business viable.

Inner ring and primary stakeholders. If we follow the inner ring clockwise, the primary stakeholders include customers, employees, suppliers, financiers (including shareholders), and communities. Their essential stakes are: receiving the promised product (customers); earning a livelihood (employees); being treated with fairness and transparency (suppliers); making profits (financiers); and paying taxes as well as other economic and social contributions (communities).

Outer ring and secondary stakeholders. The secondary stakeholders are the government, competitors, consumer advocate groups, special interest groups, and the media. Freeman does not specify their core stakes, but they may be affected by (and affect) the activities of the business. In the case of the government, this is obvious: their stake is compliance with law and the creation of value for the country. In the case of competitors, their stake would be fair competition. And so on.

Freeman says that the corporation shouldn't necessarily be in the middle of the picture, as if it were the center of the universe. He misses the point: the corporation is in the middle not because it is the center of the universe, but because it is the locus of responsibility. Being in the middle may be a privilege, but it is also a burden.

STAKEHOLDER THEORY AND CONFLICTS OF INTEREST

The stakeholder theory is the "politically correct" (and perhaps simply correct) stance on business ethics. Now, if conflicts of interest are one of the most common ethical problems in the business world, what does this theory have to say about them?

If we stick to Freeman's text, it says nothing—at least not explicitly. Freeman does not mention the concept in what is meant to be a contemporary summary of a business ethics theory he has defended for decades. The closer he gets to discussing conflicts of interest is perhaps here:

> The primary responsibility of the executive is to create as much values as possible for stakeholders. *Where stakeholder interests conflict* [emphasis added], the executive must find a way to rethink the problems so that these interests can go together, so that even more value can be created for each.[29]

For instance, if the shareholders' interest in making more money collides with the employees' interest in making more money, the executive (who, as an employee, has an interest in making more money as well) must devise a solution in which all of them end up with more money—while also furthering rather than impeding the interests of the other stakeholders (customers, suppliers, and so on).

At this point, one may venture to say that stakeholder theory, instead of ignoring conflicts of interests, deals with them continually. Let's imagine an executive who faces all kinds of interests, and whose main responsibility is to find ways to harmonize them—including, of course, her own. Here, a paradigmatic mismanaged conflict of interest would be one in which this executive favors the interest of the shareholders at the expense of the interests of the others. This would mean, for instance, firing people or reducing salaries to increase profits.

This example, though, while illustrating Freeman's point on how to manage interests in the business world, does not actually depict conflicts of interest. It instead depicts *conflicting interests*. Now, as we will see in the following chapter, conflicting interests and conflicts of interest are not the same thing. For there to be a conflict of interest, there has to be a duty involved—a duty threatened by an interest. Two interests colliding are not enough.

Despite interests being at the heart of his theory, Friedman bypasses a deeper and more common mismanagement of stakeholders' interests, as well as a more serious ethical problem in the business world: the interest or temptation of *self-dealing*.

In short, self-dealing is the act of using our job to serve our own interest (or that of a friend, family, etcetera) at the expense of the interest of our employer, client, etcetera. For example, instead of hiring the best employee, as ought to be expected, the executive hires his best friend. In Freeman's world, though, the sin of executives does not appear to be self-dealing, but shareholding dealing. Had he included, in his analysis, the problem of self-dealing, he would have been speaking of conflicts of interest as well. Why? Because all conflicts of interest involve the temptation to self-deal.[30]

A kinder reading of Freeman is to say that he is aware of the reality of self-dealing—and, with it, of conflicts of interest (How could one not?)— but that he focuses on shareholder-dealing under the assumption that self-dealing is obviously wrong.

Accordingly, there would be (paraphrasing Søren Kierkegaard[31]) "three stages of business life": those of the "self-dealer," of the "servant," and of the "leader." The first stage is one that Friedman presumably considers, and where conflicts of interest reside. The second is where shareholder dealing occurs. This is a more advanced stage than the former, but still far from ideal. The third level, finally, is the realm of stakeholder dealing. It represents the ideal, ethical attitude for executives that Freeman advocates.

SHAREHOLDER THEORY AND CONFLICTS OF INTEREST

Shareholder theory offers a sober and often misunderstood stance on business ethics, but it remains very influential—regrettably also among people who ignore or bypass the legal and ethical limits of shareholders' desires that Friedman defends. What does this say about conflicts of interest? Like the stakeholder theory, not much explicitly.

The concept, though, crops up once in Friedman's article: "The *conflict of interest* [emphasis added] is naked and clear when union officials are asked to subordinate the interest of their members to some more general purpose."[32] Now, even if the concept is almost completely absent, Friedman's moral argument about corporate social responsibility is written in the spirit of a conflict-of-interest approximation to business ethics.

We cannot justify the latter statement entirely here, to the extent that we have not defined conflicts of interest yet (that is the next chapter's burden). Let's, then, use the language of self-dealing, which, as we have mentioned, is closely tied with the concept of conflicts of interest. This will further allow us to compare, once more, Freeman and Friedman's views.

If in our interpretation of Freeman's view on conflicts of interest there are three stages of business life, in Friedman's there would be two: the first level of self-dealing (the "self-dealer") and the second of shareholder dealing (the "servant"). Furthermore, stakeholder dealing would be nothing other than a form of self-dealing.

Remember Friedman's moral argument against corporate social responsibility, and how the first premise contains the supposed primary responsibility of business executives: to increase shareholders' profits (within legal and ethical limits). As individuals, though, socially responsible executives may embrace other responsibilities, interests, agendas: animal rights, ecology, social justice, and so forth. This is all fine and laudable, as long as the executives do so with their own resources. The problem, according to Friedman, is when the same executives use shareholders' resources to pursue these ends.

To link the moral argument with self-dealing, when socially responsible executives pursue their own agenda using shareholders' money, they would not be advancing toward Freeman's third stage of business life (the "leader"), but moving backward to the first: that of the "self-dealer." We could also name the protagonist of this stage the "double-dealer"—if we want to recognize that "socially responsible" business executives do not entirely abandon their responsibility to shareholders.

The second stage of business life, from Friedman's perspective, turns out to be the ideal. Thus, the shareholder-dealing stage ought now to be renamed. Instead of corresponding to the (pejorative) "servant," this level can be said to correspond to the "employee." This, of course, is a less flashy label than "leader," but it does a nice job of reminding executives of their core status at work—and, with it, of their core responsibility: to increase profits within the limits established by law and ethics.

Of course, many business executives would rather see themselves as leaders. The term "employee," though, does not prevent anyone from being a leader. Those who are called to leadership will be leaders no matter what. The point is they should not forget their status as employees. Added to this is the fact that no executive is forbidden from becoming an entrepreneur.

Now we can see more clearly how Friedman's moral argument against corporate social responsibility is made in the spirit of conflicts of interest. He condemns what we have seen referred to here as the first stage of the business life: that of the "self-dealer" or "double-dealer." In other words, he condemns executives who, instead of doing their work-related duty, serve their own interest. As we will see in coming chapters, this equates to being in and mismanaging a conflict of interest.

TEXT BOX 2.4: FURTHER CLARIFICATIONS

In this chapter, I may have oversimplified some things—but, fear not, without betraying the essence of the theories we have discussed. It would not hurt, though, to signal these alleged over-simplifications and say something about them.

First clarification: the shareholder theory is regarded by some as a corporate social responsibility theory. In "Corporate Social Responsibility Theories," for instance, Domènec Melé includes Friedman's theory as an instance of corporate social responsibility.[33] This is valid. After all, Friedman calls his article "The Social Responsibility of Business is to Increase its Profits." Unless he is being ironic, Friedman sees his theory as a thin or minimalist form of corporate social responsibility. What he condemns are thick or maximalist versions of it.

Second clarification: Freeman is not completely committed to calling his stakeholder theory a corporate social responsibility theory. He says: "However, if stakeholder relationships are understood to be fully embedded in morality, then there is no need for an idea like corporate social responsibility [!]. We can replace it with 'corporate stakeholder responsibility.'"[34] Now, as Melé says, "in spite of these arguments, if we take CSR in a broad sense, then stakeholder theory can be considered a CSR theory, because it provides a normative framework for responsible business towards society."[35]

Third clarification: there are other corporate social responsibility theories besides the ones we have explored—theories such as "corporate social performance" and "corporate citizenship." I hope you'll excuse me for not attempting to summarize them in a few short lines. Let's just say that while the shareholder theory is rooted in economic theory, and the stakeholder theory in ethics, the others are grounded in sociology and in political theory.[36] In other words, this is what happens when economists, ethicists, sociologists, and political scientists analyze the same topic from their own perspectives.

FROM CORPORATE SOCIAL RESPONSIBILITY
TO CONFLICTS OF INTEREST

Friedman's moral argument against the stakeholder theory is not so readily dismissed. However, even if it contained one or more false premises or if it were fallacious, I see another problem with it as a business ethics theory: a problem of elitism. By this, I mean that it speaks to top business executives and not ordinary employees, who, of course, account for a majority of the business world's population. This is so to the extent that the decisions that corporate social responsibility advocates, i.e., the caring of all stakeholders, can only be made by those who "call the shots," so to speak.

Consider the matter of caring for the environment, which is part of the stake of the community. One obvious way to care for the environment is by recycling. To recycle a system must be in place, with different bins for different things: one for paper, another for batteries, one more for food waste, etc. If management does not implement this, it will be very hard, if not impossible, for employees to care for the environment in the workplace. Employees can advocate for the system all they like, but if management does not care, there is little they can do.

The same goes for caring for the stakes of the customers, suppliers, shareholders—and employees. How can an ordinary employee change things so her stakes and those of her coworkers improve? I know what you are thinking: unionize! But unions are not corporations: where they exist, they represent one, and not all, stakeholders. To this extent, corporate social responsibility does not apply to them. It is business executives who are called upon to deal in a socially responsible manner with employees and their unions.

We do not have to go to great lengths, though, to prove the elitist nature of the stakeholder theory, and of corporate social responsibility in general. Instead, one need only confirm to whom the theory is addressed—i.e., business executives—and look at the definition of "executive" in a dictionary. On the former, Freeman himself clarifies to whom the theory is targeted at the beginning of his article: "the basic idea is that businesses, *and the executives who manage them* [emphasis added], actually do and should create value for customers, suppliers, employees, communities and financiers [or shareholders]."[37] On the latter, take this definition of "executive" from *Cambridge Dictionary*: "someone in a high position, especially in business, who makes decisions and puts them into action."[38]

My point, again, is that the stakeholder theory is elitist. If it only applies to executives, this means that we would need another business ethics theory for employees. But does the shareholder theory do any better? Is it not elitist as well?

The shareholder theory, regrettably, is elitist too. Like the stakeholder theory, Friedman's theory is addressed to executives. Recall his preliminary point before he unfolds his moral argument against corporate social responsibility: the point being the need to determine who is the locus of responsibility in a corporation, and thus who is he addressing with his argument. On this, he says: "Most of the discussion of social responsibility is directed at corporations, so in what follows I shall mostly neglect the individual proprietors and speak of corporate executives."[39]

This is disappointing, since, as already noted, his article is written in the spirit of conflicts of interest. Now, the latter are anything but elitist. As Thomas L. Carson says:

> Questions about the social responsibilities of business are practical questions only for high ranking business executives. Most business people have little power or authority to make decisions about the policy issues that are discussed in the literature on the special responsibilities of business, e.g., corporate contributions to charity and corporate environmental policy. By contrast, conflicts of interest . . . are practical moral problems for almost all business people.[40]

CHAPTER SUMMARY

I began this chapter with Friedman's shareholder theory—and the corresponding critique of corporate social responsibility. Friedman contends, through a moral argument, that the main responsibility of business executives is to increase shareholders' profits, and he accuses corporate social responsibility enthusiasts of doing the opposite.

I then outlined Freeman's stakeholder theory. I did so in two stages. The first contained Freeman's descriptive and normative arguments against the shareholder theory. According to the former, improvements in law have allowed businesses to evolve to consider all stakeholders. According to the latter, there is a responsibility principle that compels businesses to take care of their stakeholders. The second stage contained Freeman's arguments for stakeholder theory. This included a new vision of business (one in which stakeholders' interests are joint) and a new responsibility for business executives: to create as much value as possible for stakeholders. The latter, Freeman justified with consequentialist, deontological, and other arguments.

I later returned to Friedman's shareholder theory to clarify that Freeman's attack may not actually land a blow on him. Why? Because Friedman's shareholder theory recognizes the authority of law and ethics.

I then discussed whether Freeman was debating with a straw man, or what was the case. We saw that Freeman was aware of Friedman's recognition of law and ethics, and so his critique of the shareholder theory addressed those who misinterpret it. This, in turn, led to a discussion of how both theories are closer than usually thought—without being identical. The main duty of executives with regard to both is still not the same.

Next, I considered the place of conflicts of interest in stakeholder theory and shareholder theory. With regard to the former, we spoke of conflicting interests as different from conflicts of interest, and of self-dealing (which equates to mismanaged conflict of interest) as a problem that Freeman either ignores or skips due to its obvious immoral status. Assuming the latter, I presented the three stages of the business life that are contained, explicitly or implicitly, in Freeman's theory: those of the "self-dealer," the "servant," and the "leader."

I thereafter suggested that the shareholder theory is written in the spirit of a conflicts-of-interest approximation to business ethics. Unable to justify this statement yet, we returned to the close concept of self-dealing and to the three stages of business life. The thesis here was that, rather than three stages, Friedman merges the first and the third, treating stakeholder theory as self-dealing. The two stages of business life, for Friedman, are those of the "self-dealer" or "double-dealer" and of the "employee."

Finally, I developed a critique that applies to both stakeholder theory and shareholder theory. This is the problem of elitism: both theories tend to address business executives, and not employees in general. This showed the need to rely on another broader and more egalitarian approximation to business ethics, which puts conflicts of interest at the core of the debate.

After all, only executives face corporate social responsibility problems, but all employees face conflicts of interest.

In between, I discussed Friedman's view of "socially responsible" shareholders and individual proprietors, Freeman's additional arguments for stakeholder theory, stakeholders' stakes, and whether or to what extent in this chapter I have oversimplified the debate around corporate social responsibility.

The term "business ethics" is used in many senses, and one of them—one that deserves far more attention—is conflicts of interest. So let's put our money where our mouth is and start discussing the concept in purity—beginning with its definition.

QUESTIONS AND EXERCISES FOR REFLECTION

1. How many arguments does Friedman present against corporate social responsibility?
2. What is the core responsibility of business executives, according to Friedman?
3. Why should executives not get carried away with corporate social responsibility, according to Friedman?
4. Explain Freeman's descriptive argument against shareholder theory.
5. Explain Freeman's normative argument against shareholder theory.
6. What is Freeman's new vision of business?
7. What is the core responsibility of business executives, according to Freeman?
8. Friedman's shareholder theory considers law and ethics. But can it be equated with stakeholder theory, and why or why not?
9. Who are the main stakeholders in a company? And what are their stakes?
10. Can you think of one stakeholder not considered by Freeman?
11. Who do you think is closer to the truth regarding the main responsibility of business executives? Friedman or Freeman? Why?
12. Explain the three stages of business life and how this links stakeholder theory with conflicts of interest.
13. What would Friedman say about conflicts of interest?
14. How does the problem of elitism affect Freeman and Friedman's stance on business ethics?
15. Can you think of other ways in which the term "business ethics" is used?

Chapter 3

DEFINING CONFLICTS OF INTEREST

What is a conflict of interest? Set this book down for a moment and draft a definition.

Now that you are done, I imagine that the task was harder than you expected. Like a nimble antelope, the concept is difficult to pin down. We usually "know" when a conflict of interest occurs, but may not *know* what exactly makes a conflict of interest what it is. So let's now try to work out a definition—and begin with two preliminary clarifications.

First, *examples are not definitions*. This we have known since the days of Socrates and Plato. Imagine that I ask you to define a table and you answer that a table is a coffee table. The latter is a good example of the former, but it is not a definition. It is an instance of a table, not its essence. Now compare that definition with the one offered by the *Webster Dictionary*: "A piece of furniture consisting of a smooth flat slab fixed on legs."[1] Better, right? This definition accurately captures the essence of tables. It is what coffee tables, accent tables, etcetera have in common. They all are pieces of furniture consisting of a smooth flat slab fixed on legs. Take out the smooth flat slat or the legs, and the table is gone. True, you can use other things as tables. For instance, you can rest your coffee on the roof of your car while putting your bag in the boot, but that does not convert your car into a table.

We must avoid the same mistake when speaking of conflicts of interest. Imagine you ask what a conflict of interest is and I reply with the following example.

The "friendly" human resources executive. Jane is a human resources executive. A position in the company has been opened, and she has been charged with filling it. The deadline is approaching and several competitive

41

candidates are applying, when something unexpected happens. Kate, her best friend, is applying too. Kate knows that she is putting Jane in trouble, but that does not make things any easier for Jane. Now Jane wonders if she should favor Kate at the expense of more qualified individuals.

This is a good example of a conflict of interest, but it is far from being a proper definition—to be so, it must show what this and other examples have in common.

Second, *counterexamples can prove a definition wrong.* Having clarified that examples do not constitute definitions, it is necessary to point out that examples, or more precisely counterexamples, have an important role when working one out. In short, I can kill a sophisticated and hard-won definition with a single bullet.

For example, let's say I redefine table as "a piece of furniture consisting of a smooth flat slab fixed on four legs" or as "a piece of furniture consisting of a slab fixed on legs." In the first case, the problem is obvious: many tables do not have four legs. One only has to provide a single example of an otherwise-legged table, and the definition is gone. In the second case, the problem is that if the slab is too rough, it will have no practical worth. Here, the counterexample will have to be produced in the imagination or, who knows, in the nearest Museum of Contemporary Art.

When counterexamples prove a definition wrong, the problem lies either in the broadness or narrowness of the definition. In the first case above, the definition was too narrow: it arbitrarily excluded things that are correctly called tables. In the second case, the definition was too broad: it arbitrarily included, in the classification of tables, things that are not.

Returning to conflicts of interest, our definition should be impervious to counterexamples, thereby hitting the mark. But we do not have to start from scratch. Philosophers before us have gone a long way in this effort. Before summoning the experts, though, let's see how far we can go by ourselves.

"CONFLICTS OF INTEREST": WHAT DOES THE LABEL SUGGEST?

Let's begin by considering what the label "conflicts of interest" suggests. If we look for a narrow, word-for-word meaning, it will merely suggest the notion of two or more interests quarreling. Whose interests? They could be anyone's—and they can even dwell within a single person. On this basis, we can construct the following (first) definition: "A conflict of interest is a situation in which two or more interests clash—a situation that can only be resolved by sacrificing one of these interests." But this is a definition that most, if not all, people will immediately reject and it is easy to show why. How? Through our tested strategy—the use of counterexamples—like the following one:

The conflicted holidaymaker. John is on holiday in Europe. He has loved his trip so far but now he has to make one last choice. He has three more days before returning home and two options, or interests, vie for position in his heart. The first one is to visit Paris; the second, to go to Rome. Eiffel Tower or the Colosseum? Baguette or pasta? Cognac or Campari? He would love to visit both but, because of time, space, and poor planning, he can only go to one. Sometimes, choosing between two goods is as hard as choosing right over a tempting wrong.

We do not have to be on holiday to suffer these kinds of problems. Choosing between two or more interests (and their corresponding goods) is part of life, but do we ever consider these situations conflicts of interest? We do not and for a reason. We do not yet know what the reason is (first we will need a clear understanding of what conflicts of interest are), but calling cases like this conflicts of interest just sounds odd. Unfolding the reason is why we are here.

The counterexample here has shown that our first definition is extremely broad. We need to narrow it down. Let's look at the label again: "conflicts of interest." I think this, to many, suggests the same thing: the interests of more than one person are in conflict, and it is difficult or even impossible to satisfy them all. Now let's try a (second) definition: "A conflict of interest is a situation in which someone's interest conflicts with the interest of someone else—a situation that can only be resolved by sacrificing one of these interests." Is this an adequate definition or is there something wrong with it as well?

It is not an adequate definition, and this can again be proved by a counterexample.

The conflicting couple. Valerie and Mark are married. They wed in the conviction that opposites attract. They are so different that if the marriage succeeds, it will be irrefutable proof that the principle is sound. But is it? Valerie likes to read; Mark, to watch TV shows. Mark likes chocolates; Valerie, gummy worms. Valerie likes the Beatles; Mark, the Rolling Stones. Their interests conflict every day—so much so that their life as a couple can be described as an endlessly recurring conflicting interest.

We all know at least one couple like this, but do we ever say that what they face regularly are conflicts of interest? Would that not also, like the case of the conflicted holidaymaker, sound odd? Personally, I have never heard the label used in these situations (and I discuss conflicts of interest for a living). What's more, I bet you haven't either. This observation should not be taken lightly, but as a strong indication that their conflicts are not, in fact, conflicts of interest. The couple face conflicts, but of another type.

This second definition is narrower than the first but still broad. Perhaps the label itself is slightly misleading. Although *conflicting interests* are a part of *conflicts of interest*, there is more to the story. But what?

TEXT BOX 3.1: DEFINING A MORAL CONCEPT: A MODEL

Efforts in the West to define moral concepts began with Socrates. His disciple Plato learned well from him, and in his dialogues he recreates his master's art.

In Plato's *Euthyphro*, for instance, Socrates searches for a definition of piety. The dialogue occurs against the backdrop of Socrates' trial—the trial that will eventually condemn him to death. Yes, defining moral concepts, as we can see, can be a matter of life or death.

This is Euthyphro's first definition: "I say that the pious is to do what I am doing now, to prosecute the wrongdoer, be it about murder or temple robbery or anything else, whether the wrongdoer is your father or your mother or anyone else; not to prosecute is impious."[2]

Socrates is not satisfied, and makes the point that examples are not definitions: "Bear in mind that I did not bid you tell me one or two of the many pious actions but that form itself that makes all pious actions pious."[3]

The dialogue continues and Euthyphro offers four more flawed definitions. Finally, he moves on from Socrates. It is our job, Plato seems to suggest, to continue the discussion.

In the *Republic*, we find the following example of the role of counterexamples in definitions. Socrates asks Polemarchus for a definition of justice. Following an earlier thinker (Simonides), Polemarchus says that justice "is just to give to each what is owed."[4]

Like in the *Euthyphro*, Socrates protests: "For plainly he doesn't mean what we were just saying—giving back to any man whatsoever something he has deposited when, of unsound mind, he demands it. And yet, what he deposited is surely owed to him, isn't it?"[5]

This is proof that counterexamples can prove a definition wrong. Justice must be defined otherwise. The rest of the *Republic* is devoted to developing that definition and, unlike the case of the *Euthyphro*, in this respect, the book reaches its aim.

CONFLICTS OF INTEREST: "X-RAYING" AN EXAMPLE

Now let's change our strategy and, instead of analyzing the label, turn our attention to good, noncontroversial examples of conflicts of interest. In fact, even if we do not know precisely what conflicts of interest are, we can still (and in fact do) agree that some cases undoubtedly belong to the category.

The general manager in love. Brandon is madly in love with Allison. All he can think about, all the time, is his new and this-time real (he tells himself) affection. He is the general manager of a hotel chain; she is an entrepreneur who markets towels. They met at the Annual Hotel Suppliers Show. By chance, Brandon's hotel is looking for a new towel supplier and several companies are bidding for the contract. Even though he has seen better options (of towel suppliers), Brandon is tempted to seal a deal with Jane.

Like the "friendly" human resources executive, this is a paradigmatic example of a conflict of interest. In fact, similar examples abound in the literature. Let's start by agreeing that this is certainly a conflict of interest, and proceed to "x-ray" the example. The procedure may reveal something that the label hides.

The scan has indeed revealed a new element. There are at play not only two interests, but a duty as well. The general manager's interest in love is at odds with that of the company he leads, but a duty is fighting his interest as well. His interest is to help his girlfriend. His duty, in turn, is to contract the best towels supplier. The interest of his employer, lastly, is also to sign up with the best towel supplier.

Perform the same x-ray on other examples and the results will be the same. In fact, this is the basic structure of all conflicts of interest: a duty fighting an interest that threatens the interest of someone else. Let's now try another (third) definition: "A conflict of interest is a situation in which an interest tempts one to disregard a duty—a situation that threatens the interest of someone else." Did we make it? Can we finish the chapter, having successfully defined conflicts of interest?

Regrettably, we are still far from the goal—to the extent that these elements are present not only in conflicts of interest but in most moral problems. In other words, like the first and second definitions, this third one is too broad, as the following counterexample makes plain.

The repentant thief. Joe, a repentant thief, is in trouble. His job search has yielded no results so far, and he is running out of money. Not only that, but the friend who has been hosting him for the last two months has given him a deadline: he must leave by the end of the week. Joe is appalled, walking home after a failed job interview, when he spots an opportunity: elderly Liza is walking alone in a dark street with a fat purse. His heart starts to run. Maybe he can do it one more time. "Until I get a job," he tells himself.

Like in the cases of the conflicted holidaymaker and the conflicting couple, we would not call this a conflict of interest—or would we? We would not, even though the three elements (an interest fighting a duty that threatens the interest of someone else) are present. Mark's interest is to steal the purse. His duty is to respect others' property. Liza's interest, ultimately, is to arrive home safely with all her belongings. What are we missing? Why is the general manager in love in a conflict of interest but not the repentant thief?

Our analysis has brought us close to an adequate definition, but there is more to do. Perhaps, it is time for what was announced at the beginning of this chapter: to summon the experts. Their insights will surely help us.

WHAT KIND OF DUTY MAKES CONFLICTS OF INTEREST SPECIAL?

Our second definition was narrower than the first, and the third, narrower than the second. Even the third, though, needs to be narrowed further. To do so, we need to establish what kind of duty and what kind of interest make conflicts of interest special. This is precisely what the experts debate—beginning with Michael Davis, who, in the early 1980s, noticed that lawyers had been discussing the topic for some time, and decided to generalize their insights to the business and professional world.

His earliest definition, dating to 1982, states that: "A person has a conflict of interest if a) he is in a relationship with another requiring him to exercise judgment in that other's service and b) he has an interest tending to interfere with the proper exercise of judgment in that relationship."[6] Travel forward thirty years and you find him presenting a similar definition:

A conflict of interest is a situation in which some person P (whether an individual or corporate body) is (1) in a relationship with another requiring P to exercise judgment on the other's behalf and (2) has a (special) interest tending to interfere with the proper exercise of judgment in that relationship.[7]

Davis does not, in his definitions, use the word "duty." This does not prevent us from identifying the duty at stake: it is not just any duty (as in our first three definitions), but a specific one: *to exercise judgment on the other's behalf*. With this, Davis significantly narrows the definition of conflicts of interest, but does he hit the mark?

Many (most?) conflicts of interest involve judgment. The general manager in love, for instance, has a duty to decide which is the best provider of towels. This is hardly a mechanical duty—the type of duty that Davis excludes from conflicts of interest. And it applies not only to selecting providers: many of the things businesspeople and professionals do—hiring workers, choosing a marketing strategy, investing money, and so on—and that are jeopardized in conflicts of interest usually involve judgment. But do they always?

Davis's main interlocutors—Neil R. Luebke, John R. Boatright, and Carson—think that they do not. They may not have changed Davis's mind, but they can change ours (provided we agree with Davis so far). How? With counterexamples. Boatright in particular has presented several that Davis himself has contested, but Carson has ventured one that remains unchallenged, and which may ultimately close the debate against Davis, namely, *the greedy stockbroker*.

> For example, suppose that in my role as a stock broker and financial advisor I advise my clients to purchase the stock of a company that I *know* will soon be facing bankruptcy, because offering this advice will promote my own financial interest or the interest of a close personal friend. Surely this is a conflict of interest, even though my *judgment* about the wisdom of this investment for my clients is not in any way impaired or made "less reliable." In some cases, conflicts of interest create temptations to do what we know will violate our duties to other parties.[8]

Davis may not have contested this counterexample, but could he? More importantly, could we? In other words, can we think of any reason to content that the greedy stockbroker does not face a conflict of interest but something else? I cannot.

We now see that Davis's proposal, regarding the duty that makes conflicts of interest special, leaves the definition too narrow. Although we are, thanks to him, closer still to an adequate definition of conflicts of interest, we cannot rest yet. What kind of duty makes them what they are, if not only exactly a duty to exercise judgment on another's behalf?

TEXT BOX 3.2: PHILOSOPHY: A BIG DIALOGUE

Even if, after Plato, philosophers wrote treatises instead of dialogues, philosophy can still be called a big, millennial dialogue (and by "millennial" I do not refer to those born between 1982 and 2004).

The discussions initiated by Socrates, and recreated by Plato in his books, have not ended. Two-and-a-half millennia later, we are still discussing many of the same topics: the essence of happiness, the limits of knowledge, the existence of the soul, the definition of beauty, and so forth. A discussion about the good life, for instance, cannot these days be undertaken seriously without bringing authors such as Aristotle and Kant to the table. In fact, the classics occupy the table—of however many legs—and we novices strive for a place at it. But we must earn the right.

Not all topics pondered (or sometimes, truth be told, fought over) in philosophy are ancient, though. Conflicts of interest is, comparatively, a very new one. This does not mean that people did not face conflicts of interest in ancient Greece or Medieval London—they certainly did. But for reasons that are yet to be discovered, the label "conflicts of interest" and the academic dialogue around it started late, in the twentieth century.

If we presume to join the philosophers at their discussion around the table, we should not do so simply to interrupt or to impose our half-formed idea of what conflicts of interest, but, first of all, to learn.

Only then, after the experts have shared their opinion with us, may we give ours—but only, of course, under the condition that we have something worth saying. And it bears repeating: first we need to listen and learn. So how do the masters of conflicts of interest define the concept? And who is closest to the truth? This is precisely what we are now looking at.

A (FIDUCIARY) DUTY TO ACT IN THE INTEREST OF ANOTHER?

Davis's 1982 article drew a response from Luebke (1987). Like Davis, Luebke does not use the word "duty" when discussing conflicts of interest, but we can infer its identity:

> Any person or organised group capable of deliberate judgment or action and who acts or is empowered to act in a fiduciary role can have a CI

[conflict of interest] . . . I use "fiduciary" here in a broad sense . . . to connote any party in whom trust or reliance is reposed for the purpose of advising, aiding, acting on behalf of, or protecting the interest of another party.[9]

The duty, thus, would be a *fiduciary duty to advise, aid, act on behalf of, or protect the interest of another party*. In this way, Luebke includes but transcends the category of judgment. Carson's greedy stockbroker, for instance, fits here, since he was entrusted to advise his clients financially—a duty that, as seen, does not always demand judgment.

If we look more closely at duty as implied by, though, it seemingly misses the mark as well. In what way? Let's offer another example.

The babysitting brother. The weekend arrives and Adam has no plans. His sister Amy, on the other hand, is going to a wedding. Amy asks him if he can take care of her four kids and he accepts. Once the kids arrive, though, his date, Eve, calls. Eve wants to meet and talk about their relationship, and the encounter has to happen now. Adam can't help but get agitated (rarely do such urgent meetings have a positive outcome), but hesitates. After all, if Eve comes, he will be very distracted, and thus less apt to protect the interests of his nieces and nephews.

This example shows that Luebke's duty leaves his definition of conflicts of interest too broad. The babysitting brother is in a fiduciary relationship[10] and has an interest that jeopardizes the corresponding duty, but we would not say that he faces a conflict of interest. Truth be told, Luebke excludes such private cases from conflicts of interest, but for the wrong reason—because of the intangible nature of the interest (as we will see).

When Boatright joined the debate in 1992, he included the word "obligation" (a synonym of duty) in his definition of conflicts of interest, thus facilitating their understanding. But what kind of obligation? Consider this assertion from Boatright in 2008: "[For a conflict of interest to exist,] first, there must be an obligation to act in the interest of another."[11]

Like in Luebke's case, his proposal regarding duty is close to the target but still open to criticism. In fact, if Luebke's version of duty made the definition of conflicts of interest too broad, Boatright's leaves it even broader. In short, the *duty to act in the interest of another* is not, as was the case with Luebke, expressly restricted to fiduciary relationships. The problem is that the duty to act in the interest of another can be broadly interpreted to include, for instance, the duty we all have to aid people in extreme need. Immediately after, Boatright clarifies that "this kind of obligation is characteristic of fiduciaries, agents, and professionals,"[12] but this is not to say that it excludes other cases. A charitable interpretation would be that Boatright is discussing conflicts of interest exclusively in the business world, but the duty to aid those in need certainly applies in business contexts as well. This is the case of *the stingy CEO*, who faces a moral problem but not a conflict of interest.

The stingy CEO. Leonardo is the CEO of a company. Christmas is approaching and, like every year, some workers are organizing a fundraiser. The purpose of the fundraiser this year is to buy toys for kids from a poor area of town. The CEO is promoting the fundraiser at every opportunity. Still, he personally has not donated a single penny; donations are anonymous and he is very stingy. He has a moral duty to aid those in need, but his stinginess is making it difficult to honor this duty.

HITTING THE TARGET? A JOB-RELATED DUTY

Perhaps, the best account of the duty in question is Carson's. As he argued in 2004, in order for a conflict of interest to exist, "1. There must be an individual (*I*) who has duties to another party (P) in virtue of holding an office or a position."[13] In other words, the duty at stake in a conflict of interest is an *office or position-related duty.*

If we look again at the few examples of conflicts of interest presented in this chapter, we will find that in each there is an office or position-related duty at play. The "friendly" human resource executive has a duty to hire the best candidates; the general manager in love, a duty to choose the best supplier; and the greedy stockbroker, a duty to recommend sound stocks. Now consider the following series of examples of conflicts of interest (extracted from the works of Davis, Luebke, Boatright, and Carson) and evaluate whether the case is the same.

A bank president considers authorizing a loan to a friend who will soon face bankruptcy. A business executive is inclined to recommend a contract that is disadvantageous to his employer but beneficial to himself. A trust administrator ponders investing funds in a company that he owns. An accountant offers to moonlight for a competing employer. A stockbroker thinks of churning her client's accounts. An advertiser has the chance to bring in a new client whose product competes with that of a former client. A personnel officer is inclined to hire a person who saved her father's life. An executive uses his influence to scale up his department's bureaucracy and, in so doing, gain more power in the organization. An employee resists new technology that will render her skills and knowledge obsolete.

A general manager refuses to change the failing policies of his company because he designed these policies. A broker is moved to select an inferior security because it generates a higher commission. An executive owns stocks in a supplier to her company. Etcetera.

Like in the earlier examples, the duties at stake in all these cases are office or position related—which one may as well call, for the sake of further clarity and simplicity, work or job related, or simply job duties.[14] There is a duty to allocate loans to individuals who will repay them, another to recommend beneficial contracts to one's employer, and so on.

Carson's thesis is very promising, but are we sure it is flawless? The best way to test this is with the strategy we have been using again and again in this chapter: the use of counterexamples. We would have to come up with a good instance of a conflict of interest that escapes this type of duty, or with another case that does fit with it but is not a conflict of interest. Or both. I cannot think of one, can you? If you can, you may be in a position to make a strong contribution to this debate.

Besides its seeming immunity against counterexamples, Carson's account has two practical advantages over the others. First, it facilitates the identification of conflicts of interest. All that is now required is a clear notion of what one's job-related duties are (something one can find in a contract, job description, etcetera), as well as the most common interests that hinder the honoring of those duties.

Second, Carson's account makes rationalization harder. Rationalization is the power to deceive oneself with regard to the morality of one's actions. Deep down I know that what I am doing is wrong, yet I tell myself that it is not all that bad or even not bad at all. One way of doing this is by saying to myself that what I am facing is not a conflict of interest, when in fact I am. Since their identification is easy, the chances of rationalization decrease.

TEXT BOX 3.3: SCHWAB'S EXPANSION OF DAVIS' DEFINITION

In "Defining Conflicts of Interest in Terms of Judgment" (2019), Abraham P. Schwab joins Davis in arguing that the duty at stake in conflicts of interest is always a duty to exercise judgment on another's behalf. Schwab's definition, though, is broader to the extent that he defines judgment in a broader way than Davis does.

According to Davis, judgment is "the capacity to make correctly decisions not as likely to be made correctly by a simple clerk with a book of rules and access to all the facts (and only the facts) the actual decision maker has. Judgment implies discretion."[15] The clerk can doubtless be tempted to disregard the mechanical duties contained in the "rulebook" (and thus face a moral problem), but since following this book does not require judgment, Davis believes that the clerk does not face a conflict of interest.

Schwab thinks that this exclusion is arbitrary:

> First, existing rules are neither necessary nor sufficient to define what one ought to do. That some act or judgment does or does not follow the rules may or may not mark a moral difference. Second, rules require interpretation in their implementation. Davis's clerk with a book of rules . . . must make a judgment about how and when to enforce the rules. . . . The agent who works on behalf of an employer must determine what that work requires of them at each given moment and throughout the day.[16]

I agree with Schwab that mechanical duties sometimes involve judgment, but do they always? Clearly not. When they do not, would Schwab, like Davis, reject the existence of a conflict of interest? This seems necessary. But what about Carson's greedy stockbroker? Would not Schwab want to say that he is in a conflict of interest?[17]

ON INTEREST: BEGINNING THE DISCUSSION

Having identified the type of duty at stake, our (fourth) definition of conflicts of interest now reads as follows: "A conflict of interest is a situation in which an interest tempts one to disregard an office-, position-, work-, or job-related duty—a situation that threatens the interest of someone else." Now it is time to evaluate the first interest, i.e., the one that threatens the duty. Should we also restrict it to a certain type?

This question can be restated as follows: Do intangible interests (like friendship or love) correspond to conflicts of interest or is it only tangible ones (like money or real estate) that do? In the debate around duty, it was Davis who provided the narrowest account, but when it comes to interest it is Luebke who claims the honor:

> By "interest" I do not mean an interest in the psychological sense of
> a feeling or desire. . . . Interest, as I define the term, refers to some
> material right, benefit, asset, or share possessed by the fiduciary or
> by others with whom he/she is legally or closely associated (fam-
> ily members, business partners, employer, benefactor, client, or the
> like).[18]

Many conflicts of interest, in fact, involve tangible interests; take the following case.

The acquisitive financial analyst. Louis is a financial analyst. His contract
requires him to recommend financial investments to management. After
some research, he compiles some of the best options in the market. He feels
tempted, though, to include, among the options, a company his family co-
owns. As a matter of fact, the company is currently looking for investors.
He strongly believes that his family's company has a big future, but that
future has yet to come.

This case shows a job duty (give the best financial advice) and an
interest (money through his family company) that conflicts with the duty
and threatens the interest of someone else (his employer). The acquisitive
financial analyst does indeed face a conflict of interest, but do they always
involve tangible interests, as Luebke argues?

Not really. Remember the "friendly" human resources executive and
the general manager in love. They faced conflicts of interest and their interests were intangible ones. Now consider the following example, a slight
variation of the acquisitive financial analyst:

The nationalist financial analyst. Marjorie is a foreign financial analyst
working in the United States. Her contract requires her to recommend
financial investments to management. After some research, she compiles
some of the best options in the market. She feels tempted, though, to
include, among the options, a company from her country. She finally finds
one that is currently looking for investors. The company is doing well, but
not quite as well as the other ones. Still, she hesitates.

Is Marjorie in a conflict of interest? Yes. There is a work-related duty
(to give sound financial advice) and an intangible interest (nationalism) that
is in conflict with the duty and that threatens the interest of someone else
(her employer). Why wouldn't we call this a conflict of interest? As a matter of fact, a lot of conflicts of interest involve intangible interests, but why?
What is behind this?

Posing more examples will not settle the issue. After all, we may be
mistaken in calling the cases conflicts of interest. To find the answer, we
have to analyze the structure of moral problems in general. First, though,

let's review what the other scholars say. Luebke's account of interest has proven to be too narrow so we need to expand it.

BEYOND TANGIBLE INTERESTS

Luebke's position is unusual. Compare his position with that of Davis, who from the beginning admitted intangible interests in conflicts of interest:

> "Interest" should be interpreted broadly to include all those influences, loyalties, concerns, emotions or the like that can make (competent) judgment less reliable than it might otherwise be (without making it incompetent). Thus, even moral constraints . . . may be interests for the purposes of this analysis.[19]

In his 1987 paper, Luebke criticized Davis for rendering, through this broad definition, "the category of CI far larger than the bounds of standard or effective usage."[20] As counterexamples, he presented two cases. First, that of a parent postponing a medical treatment for his child out of a desire to go on holiday. Second, that of an estate agent failing to show a house to a potential buyer because of an aversion to his accent. None of these cases would be conflicts of interest, in Luebke's opinion.

Davis responded to the first case by saying that the parent was indeed in a conflict of interest. He has not, to my knowledge, referred to the second, but if the first is a conflict of interest, the second would be so even more categorically. Who is right on this one?

Neither is right, I think. Luebke is correct in thinking that the parent is not in a conflict of interest, but for the wrong reason. The parent is not in a conflict of interest because his paternal duty is not an office, position, work-, or job-related duty (and not because, as Luebke thinks, of the intangible nature of the interest). Now, if the parent is not in a conflict of interest, then Davis is wrong as well.

And what about the estate agent? If intangible interests correspond to conflicts of interest, as I will argue soon, he will indeed be in one. This is so to the extent that the duty involved is a job duty.

Boatright, for his part, in 1992 was inclined to restrict interests to tangible ones:

> Roughly, a person has an interest in something when the person stands to gain some benefit or advantage from that thing. . . . The benefit or advantage is usually restricted to a financial gain of some kind and should

be limited to something tangible. Merely satisfying a desire, for example, would not seem to be enough, for otherwise a lawyer who detests a client and secretly hopes that the client will be convicted would face a conflict of interest, as would a lawyer who prefers to play golf rather than spend the time adequately representing a client.[21]

Now compare that with this piece from 2008: "The interest that interferes is usually some prospective financial gain, but it can be anything that a person values, such as family well-being or public recognition."[22] Clearly, Boatright changed his mind. He does not seem to be a huge fan of intangible interest, though—only one out of the six examples of conflicts of interest he offers in this last piece involves an intangible interest (that of the judge):

> A physician . . . orders a test from a lab in which he or she is an investor; a judge hears a case in which a family member is a party; an executive owns stock in a supplier of her or his company; an accountant audits a company in which he or she holds stock; the administrator of a trust invests funds in a company she or he owns; and an insurance broker is paid commissions by the insurer he or she recommends.[23]

TEXT BOX 3.4: INTERESTS: A COMPLEMENTARY OBSERVATION

The *Merriam-Webster Dictionary* defines "interest" as "1 a: a feeling that accompanies or causes special attention to an object or class of objects."[24] Now if interests are feelings, they must be intangible, or have you ever touched one? Interests reside in people's "hearts," so to speak. But if this is the case, why do we speak of tangible interests?

This is the thing. When we speak of an interest that is tangible or intangible, we are not referring to the interest itself, but to the object of our interest. But what makes something tangible? The same dictionary defines tangible as "1 a: capable of being perceived especially by the sense of touch."[25] For instance, I am interested in money. Is my interest tangible? It is to the extent that money is tangible (and please do not get me started on cryptocurrency). The same goes for things like houses, cars, gold, and so on. My interest in love, on the contrary, is not tangible because love itself is not. Or have you ever touched or seen a father's love for his son? You have seen acts of love, but not love itself.

The difference between tangible and intangible interests, thus, lies in the tangible or intangible nature of the thing that interests us. A tangible interest, then, is an interest in something tangible; an intangible interest, an interest in something intangible.

Now consider this. Some things are of such a nature that they can awaken both tangible and intangible interests. For instance, I can be interested in a painting for its market value. I buy it and store it in a bank. In this case, I am interested in the tangible dimension of the painting. If my interest instead lies in the beauty the painting contains, then it qualifies as intangible. The same goes for humans. For instance, when a man sees a woman as a sexual object, his interest is tangible. If he sees her as the love of his life, though, his interest happens to be intangible—or tangible and intangible, since he still wants to kiss her.

EXPANDING INTERESTS FURTHER

Of all the authors, it is Carson who broadens the category of interest as far as reason allows. He does so in two ways. First, he includes, among the interests that can create a conflict of interest, that of harming (and not only of promoting) the interest of someone else.[26] Second, he also includes animals among the other parties whose interests one may be interested in affecting.[27] Let's consider an example for each—but now from the self-employed world.

The broken-hearted photographer. Lara is a freelance photographer. She has been recently hired to take pictures for a child's birthday party. After some negotiations with the mother, she committed to do the job. Everything was fine until the day arrived. She went along to the address she'd been given but as soon as the door was opened, she froze: the dad was Peter, an ex-boyfriend who left her heartbroken some years ago. Nobody had noticed the connection. A dark interest emerged: to do a bad job with the pictures.

As we can see, Lara faces a conflict of interest. She has a work-related duty (to take photographs) and an interest that interferes with it (a desire to harm an ex-boyfriend). If she yields to the interest, she will hurt Peter and his family's interest in turn.

The resentful dog walker. Caitlin is a dog walker. One of her clients has a dog named Tyson. Last weekend Tyson bit her and other dogs in a chaotic incident. Caitlin became resentful, but instead of walking away from the contract, an idea came to her. She was walking the dogs one morning when they reached an avenue. Cars were going fast in both directions, and she felt the temptation to set Tyson free. "That way Tyson will hurt no one anymore," she told herself. But deep down, she wanted revenge.

Caitlin's job duty is to walk dogs. Her interest is to hurt Tyson. Tyson's interest is to be walked—an interest that his master shares. Caitlin faces a conflict of interest as well.

These cases show that any interest can create conflicts of interest; but why? An argument is due for the inclusion of intangible interests.

As we saw in chapter 1, most serious moral problems involve a moral duty fighting an interest (a need, inclination, etcetera). Any interest, as long as it tempts us, qualifies. This is because immorality occurs when we act against a moral duty, regardless of what interest pulled us in that direction—in the direction of lying, stealing, and so forth. I may have a very bizarre inclination to act against a moral duty, but if I honor the latter, all will be (ethically speaking) fine. If I do not, however, my inclination will not excuse me—like in the next case.

The superstitious philanthropist. Mary is an active philanthropist. She loves humanity and is always open to helping people. Mary is also very superstitious and this has led her to some unusual situations. While walking home, Jessica, an elderly woman, asks for help. She needs someone to carry her groceries into her flat, which is located on the thirteenth floor. The problem? The number thirteen is a signal of bad luck. Mary considers walking away, but her sense of duty pushes her in the other direction.

As a class of moral problems, conflicts of interest have the same basic structure: when, in a conflict of interest, we are tempted by an interest to disregard a duty. Now, since what matters, morally speaking, is that we do what duty commands, the tangible or intangible nature of the interest does not make any significant difference. Several examples presented in this chapter (the "friendly" human resources executive, the general manager in love, among others) illustrate this point, and so our fourth definition does not need to be revised.

CHAPTER SUMMARY

I began this chapter with a reflection on what a definition demands. Inspired by Socrates and Plato, I showed how examples are not definitions and how counterexamples can prove a definition wrong. While the former saved us from committing a common mistake, the latter gave us a way to test whether a definition was unduly narrow or unduly broad.

Next, I focused on the label "conflicts of interest" and proposed two preliminary definitions that saw conflicts of interest as conflicting interests. These definitions were too broad, as the conflicted holidaymaker and the conflicting couple illustrated.

After analyzing the label, I changed the strategy and "x-rayed" a good example of a conflict of interest: the general manager in love. This revealed that conflicts of interest do involve at least two people with conflicting interests (as the second definition suggested), but a duty as well. This inspired a third definition that, nevertheless, happened to be unduly broad again; it described moral problems in general, and not just conflicts of interest. The repentant thief confirmed this point.

At this stage in the chapter, I summoned Davis, Luebke, Boatright, and Carson, who taught us the route to arriving at a definition: specifying the duty and the interest at stake.

I then turned to duty, gathering and analyzing four accounts: (a) duty to exercise judgment on another's behalf (Davis [and Scwhab]), (b) fiduciary duty to advise, aid, act on behalf of, or protect the interest of another party (Luebke), (c) business or professional duty to act in the interest of another (Boatright), and (d) office or position-related duty (Carson).

The first account was shown to be too narrow by the greedy stockbroker, which illustrated that conflicts of interest do not always involve judgment. The second account was broader but excessively so, as the babysitting brother made clear. The third account was likewise too broad, as underlined by the philanthropic CEO. This left us with the fourth account, which I defended on three grounds: it appears immune to counterexamples, it facilitates the identification of conflicts of interest, and it hinders rationalization. This account of duty led to a fourth definition of conflicts of interest.

The final task was to analyze whether there was a need to restrict the concept of interest as well. In other words, should we include, in conflicts of interest, tangible and intangible interests, or only the former? Luebke argued that we should restrict the classification to tangible interests, but the "friendly" human resource executive, the general manager in love, and the nationalist financial analyst cautioned against this.

If Luebke restricted interests in conflicts of interest to tangible ones, Davis, Boatright, and Carson include them. The verdict? The latter approach. The reason is that, morally speaking, what matters in conflicts of interest is that duty be honored, regardless of what tempts us otherwise. The broken-hearted photographer and the resentful dog walker illustrate that even hate, and hate for an animal, can create conflicts of interest.

In the midst of all this, I discussed Socrates' strategy for defining things, philosophy as a big dialogue, Schwab's insistence on defining duty in terms of judgment, and what makes an interest intangible.

So, what is a conflict of interest? *A conflict of interest is a situation in which an interest tempts one to disregard an office-, position-, work,- or job-related duty—a situation that threatens the interest of someone else.* Do you disagree? Put this book down and draft your own definition. You should now be much better equipped to do so than when we started the chapter.[28]

QUESTIONS AND EXERCISES FOR REFLECTION

1. Think of a former or current job and share a past or present conflict of interest (if you do not work yet, research typical conflicts of interest in your preferred future occupation).
2. Identify the closest business to where you are right now (a coffee shop, a petrol station, or whatever it may be). Consider the people working there and imagine at least one conflict of interest in their lives.
3. Our first definition of conflicts of interest regarded them as conflicting interests. Given this definition, we saw the cases of the conflicted holidaymaker and the conflicting couple. Present another example.
4. In our struggle to define conflicts of interests, we "x-rayed" an example: the general manager in love. Think of another example of a conflict of interest and do the same (i.e., identify the duty, the interest that threatens the duty, and the threatened interest).
5. Davis defines the duty that belongs to conflict of interest as a duty to exercise judgment on another's behalf. Share two examples of conflicts of interest: one in which a judgment is at play and another in which there is no judgment involved. If you agree with Davis that conflicts of interest always involve judgment, defend your position.
6. Carson defines the duty that belongs to conflict of interest as office or position related. Is he right? Can you think of a counterexample? If not, review your former examples and explain whether they confirm Carson's definition.
7. Present two additional examples of conflicts of interest: the first involving a tangible interest and the second, an intangible one.
8. Return to questions 1 and 2. Take the examples you offered and identify the duties at stake and the interests that make their performance difficult. Now evaluate: Were they good examples of conflicts of interest? Why?

Chapter 4

CLASSIFYING CONFLICTS OF INTEREST

L et's do a magic trick, one in which you will travel through time and space (I am writing this book from a faraway place in the past). I will ask you to think of a conflict of interest and I will tell you (without knowing the example you have in mind) what kind of conflict of interest it is. Go ahead.

Have you finished? Do not forget your example. We will return to this trick at the end of the chapter. But you need to read the whole chapter; otherwise, the trick will not work. And what will we look at in this chapter? Classifying conflicts of interests.

Why (beyond the fun of the trick) do we need to devote a chapter to this classification? We need it to continue mastering our object of study. This would be the case if we were studying planets, birds or—to mention another moral "thing"—virtue. Since this is a book about ethics, let's focus on the latter and show how classifying a moral concept strengthens its understanding and, thus, facilitates its mastery.

Let's begin with a definition. What is a virtue? According to Aristotle's definition in the *Nicomachean Ethics*,[1] a virtue or excellence is a quality that allows a thing to perform its function or purpose well and, thus, to attain its highest good. For instance, the virtue of a fruit tree is fruitfulness. If a fruit tree is fruitful, it will perform its function, which is to produce fruits, well. In this way, the fruit tree attains its highest good. Now think of a clock. The virtue of a clock is precision. When a clock is precise, it performs its function, which is to measure and indicate time, well. In this way, like the fruit tree, the clock attains its highest good. Next think of an occupation: selling. The virtue of the seller is persuasion. A seller who possesses this virtue sells a lot, i.e., performs her function well and, in this way, attains a seller's highest good. But what is human's function (that which only humans do or that which no other being does as well)? To use and follow reason. Thus, a human quality will be a virtue if it allows humans to perform their function well and, in turn, to attain their highest good.

So far we have a definition of virtue, but we would surely benefit from a classification of virtues. In fact, this would allow us to understand, in a more concrete way, what virtues are.

Aware of the value of a classification, Aristotle himself organizes virtues into two classes: intellectual and moral. Intellectual virtues help us to perform our function well (and thus to attain our highest good) by imposing order on our thoughts. Think of theoretical wisdom, the intellectual virtue that allows us to reason our way to the truth. Or of practical wisdom (prudence), which allows us to reason our way to wise choices.

Moral virtues, in turn, help us to perform our function well (and thus to attain our highest good) by imposing order on our feelings and desires. Courage, for instance, imposes order on fear, a feeling. Self-control, in turn, imposes order on our desire for food.

Aristotle lists and analyses many virtues. Beyond those mentioned above, he studies justice, generosity, gentleness, friendliness, and wittiness, etcetera. After Aristotle, Plato-inspired tradition took a step forward in the classification of the virtues, identifying four cardinal or fundamental virtues: prudence, justice, fortitude, and temperance. Christian ethics, in turn, eventually added to the list three theological virtues: faith, hope, and love. In this way, premodern ethics speak of seven fundamental virtues that are necessary to reach our highest good.

Now, just as the classification of virtues aids our understanding of virtue, so too will the classification of conflicts of interest. This enhanced understanding will, in turn, improve our ability to identify conflicts of interest—and to avoid overlooking whole classes of them. This is the burden of this chapter.

FORMAL AND INFORMAL CONFLICTS OF INTEREST

Let's begin by discussing *formal* and *informal* conflicts of interest. The distinction is found in an example that Davis presents in his ground-breaking essay of 1982: that of a bull breeder.[2]

The competitive bull breeder. A person (let's call him Max) raises Black Angus bulls for some cattle show. A clueless competitor (let's call him John) asks Max to look after his own bulls while he is away: check the temperature if one looks weak, bring them in if a storm approaches, and so on. Max accepts but almost immediately feels inclined to be less diligent than expected in his duties of care. His interest in winning the cattle show clouds his judgment.

Davis presents this as an instance of a conflict of interest. The point he makes is that not only formal roles (like that of a lawyer) but also mere informal relationships (like the role Max assumes when accepting helping John) can be subject to conflicts of interest. If we were to classify Davis's insight, we might call it an informal conflict of interest. But is he right? Is Max in a conflict of interest? More importantly, is it proper to speak of informal conflicts of interest or do only formal ones exist?

Let's first discuss whether Max, the competitive bull breeder, is in a conflict of interest. He is clearly in a conflict, but is the duty at stake an office-, position-, work-, or job-related one? The latter, as we have discussed, seem quintessential to conflicts of interests. Now, Max has a duty borne of a promise—namely, to look after John's bulls, but this promise has not put Max in an office or a job. He is just a bull breeder who has made a promise to an acquaintance. He has a duty to take due care of John's bulls, but it is an ordinary duty. Thus, his interest in winning the cattle show puts Max in an ordinary moral problem, not a conflict of interest.

The case would be different if Max, in addition to raising bulls, worked for or held a position in the organization that is arranging the cattle show. As co-organizer of the contest, he might well be subject to some temptations and, thus, to conflicts of interest; for instance, deciding to compete despite his role as co-organizer. As a mere competitor, though, he is not in a conflict of interest. He has duties as a competitor, such as that of fair play, but these duties are not the type of duties that create conflicts of interest.

Does this mean that we should not speak of informal conflicts of interest? Not necessarily. We can deny that Max is in a formal conflict of interest and still recognize the existence of the informal type—meaning nothing more than conflicts of interest that occur within informal organizations or in informal business relationships.

Not every organization and business is formal. At any given time, there are millions of informal entities and deals in the world, especially in the so-called "developing" one. It would be preposterous to deny both their existence and the conflicts of interest that occur around them. Consider this example.

The "informal" entrepreneur. Javier is an excellent tour guide. When his friends or family visit him, he takes them to the best spots in town. Conscious of this, he decides to charge for his services to earn a side income—but does not (yet) have the required authorization or permit. One day, the owner of a local restaurant approaches him: "If you take the tourists to my place, I will give you unlimited free lunches." He knows of better restaurants to show his customers but still hesitates. After all, who does not like free lunches?

Javier is in an informal conflict of interest: he has an "informal" work-related duty with his casual clients and an interest that threatens that duty and the interest of his clients. Despite being right, Davis chose the wrong example.

TEXT BOX 4.1: THE PROBLEM WITH EXPANDING INFORMAL CONFLICTS OF INTEREST FURTHER

Those of you who have not been convinced by the definition of conflicts of interest favored in this book (which restricts conflicts of interest to situations in which an office-, position-, work-, or job-related duty is at stake) may wish to defend the inclusion of more informal conflicts of interest—and not just those that occur within informal businesses and organizations. You might insist, for instance, that the competitive bull breeder faces a conflict of interest. And you might add (even more controversially) that the conflicted parent who we discussed last chapter (when analyzing "interest") would be in a conflict of interest as well. And so on.

The conflicted parent, let's recall, had a duty to take his son to a doctor's appointment. He also had an interest to go on holiday. The interest clouded his judgment and thus put him in a conflict of interest. Or so Davis says.[3]

The problem with admitting cases like this as conflicts of interest has been pointed out by Luebke: doing so would "render the category of CI [conflicts of interest] far larger than the bounds of standard effective usage."[4] In fact, do we ever use the term outside the business and professional world? Do we ever use it to describe conflicts that occur in private life? We do not. Now, Davis may say that we should start doing so. The question, then, is how this helps anything. He may answer that it is not a matter of utility, but of accuracy. In other words, even if it makes no practical difference, it is accurate to include these as cases of conflicts of interest, and hence we should do so. But the fact that we do not use the term in private contexts, I think, is a strong indication that there is something odd about taking this approach.

A last observation: Davis's talk of duties to exercise judgment on another's behalf has a dual effect—it excludes real conflicts of interest from the category (for example, the greedy stockbroker) and includes, as conflicts of interests, situations that are not.

POTENTIAL AND ACTUAL CONFLICTS OF INTEREST

This distinction we also owe to Davis. In his 1982 article, inspired by the "ABA Code of Professional Responsibility," Davis spoke of *potential, latent,* and *actual* conflicts of interest. By 2012, though, he had simplified this by leaving out the latent type (under further scrutiny, the distinction between potential and latent is a little stretched):

> A conflict of interest is potential if and only if P has a conflict of interest with respect to a certain judgment but is not yet in a situation in which he must make that judgment. Potential conflicts of interest, like time bombs, may or may not go off. A conflict of interest is actual if and only if P has a conflict of interest with respect to a certain judgment and is in a situation in which he must make the judgment.[5]

In this book, I have argued that conflicts of interest are not restricted to duties to exercise judgment on another's behalf, but Davis's distinction between the potential and actual types is not affected by this. We would only have to rephrase the former definitions as follows: "A conflict of interest is potential if and only if P has a conflict of interest with respect to a certain office-, position-, work-, or job-related duty but is not yet in a situation in which she must actualise that duty. Potential conflicts of interest, like time bombs, may or may not go off. A conflict of interest is actual if and only if P has a conflict of interest with respect to a certain office-, position-, work-, or job-related duty and is in a situation in which she must actualise that duty."

Consider the following example of a potential conflict of interest.

The lovestruck supplier. Clark and Lana are dating. Clark is a supply chain manager at the best supermarket in town; Lana, an entrepreneur who just launched a new frozen product. Naturally, Lana wants to place her product at Clark's work. For that, though, a spot needs to open, so she needs to be patient. It is when a spot for a new product opens up that Clark will have to make a decision—one that, in this case, will require judgment. What will he do when that day arrives?

Is Clark in a conflict of interest? Not entirely. He does not yet have to decide which new frozen product is to be admitted to the supermarket. Thus, the proper thing to do is to speak of a potential, instead of an actual, conflict of interest. To be able to speak of an actual conflict of interest, circumstances must change.

Continuing with the example, the conflict will become actual if the spot for a new frozen product opens up and Lana decides to offer her product. Here, Clark will have an interest in choosing Lana's product. But there might (though not necessarily) be a better product in the market, in which case the selection of Lana's one would hurt the company, as sales would be slower and lower than if the better alternative were chosen. As a result, Clark will be in a situation in which an interest makes it difficult for him to do his job well. He will be in an actual conflict of interest.

Of course, a potential conflict of interest is not destined to become an actual one. Here is how this could happen in our example: (1) The spot never opens up; (2) The spot opens up but Lana decides not to present her product, perhaps to save Clark a conflict of interest; (3) Lana and Clark break up; (4) The supermarket closes or Lana's business dies due to, say, a pandemic; (5) Clark changes position within the company; (6) Clark is fired or changes job. And so on.

The above example reinforces the idea that potential conflicts of interest should not be treated as if they were actual. An actual conflict of interest demands management; a potential one does not. The most a potential one can demand is anticipation, so as to secure timely and proper management when it actualizes.

REAL AND APPARENT CONFLICTS OF INTEREST

A third distinction in the classification of conflicts of interest, first proposed by Luebke (who in turn takes the idea from codes of ethics), is that of *apparent* conflicts of interest.[6] As the name suggests, they are not *real* conflicts of interest, but why exactly?

If a conflict of interest is a situation in which an interest tempts us to disregard an office-, position-, work-, or job-related duty (a situation that also threatens the interest of someone else), one may say that the apparent type is one in which either the interest does not exist or the duty is not the right kind. Let's analyze this.

The latter would be the case of the competitive bull breeder. Some may think that he is in a conflict of interest, but if conflicts of interest only happen when there is an office- or work-related duty involved, then this case does not qualify. Rather, the bull breeder is facing an ordinary moral problem.

Of course, when codes of ethics speak of apparent conflicts of interest, commanding their avoidance, they do not have *this kind* of apparent conflict of interest in mind. Leaders of businesses and organizations are not worried about their workers making this kind of theoretical mistake. What they want is for employees to avoid situations that might lead others to think they are not doing their job properly, even if this is not the case.

When writers of codes of ethics refer to apparent conflicts of interest, they have in mind those that involve apparent interests: there is a position- or work-related duty involved, and the person is apparently tempted by an interest to dishonor this duty.

Smith the smith. John Smith leads The Smith Factory, a company that treats metals. He is currently looking for a new smith when, among the applicants, a candidate named Jane Smith pops up. Jane is the best candidate, but, when John recommends that she be hired, everybody at the Smith Factory looks at him with suspicion: he couldn't be hiring a relative, could he? The fact is that John and Jane are not related at all. They just share the same last name. John, thus, is not in a conflict of interest.

Smith is a common last name, but I could not resist using it for the example. Let's say that the last name is rare: Contavalli, for instance. In that case, it would be reasonable for other workers to suspect that John is in a conflict of interest. John Smith (now John Contavalli) would be in an apparent conflict of interest, not in a real one. Why? Because there is no interest tempting him to hire someone other than the best candidate for the position.

Since these are not situations in which an interest tempts us to disregard an office, position-, work-, or job-related duty, apparent conflicts of interest are not problematic in the same way that conflicts of interest are. I am not going to spoil the next chapter (which asks why conflicts of interest are morally problematic), but since apparent conflicts of interest are not real conflicts of interest, we can freely explain why they are morally problematic without spoiling anything.

As Davis says, apparent conflicts of interest are problematic ("objectionable" is the word he uses) "for the same reason that any merely apparent wrongdoing is objectionable. It misleads people about their security, inviting unnecessary anxiety and precaution."[7] In the case of Smith the smith (or, indeed, that of Smith's alter ego Contavalli), hiring Jane Smith will create anxiety, wariness, and, in general, a bad environment within the company. "Why is John Smith serving his family? Is he not supposed to serve the company? Is Jane the best candidate?," coworkers will ask, even though John in fact hired the best person.

So, what should one do in these cases? If evading the situation is not possible or practicable, the next step is to explain how there is no conflict of interest at all. In the case of Smith the smith, this could be done through an email showing both family trees.

TEXT BOX 4.2: META CONFLICTS OF INTEREST?

In "Comparing Conflicts of Interest Across the Professions," Andrew Stark suggests the existence of *meta* conflicts of interest:

> Consider Michael Pritchard's example of "Adam," a professional of undersigned profession who "is invited to play golf with some friends on a particular beautiful day" at a time when he has "an appointment with a client." Pritchard believes that Adam's circumstance does not even rise to a "potential conflict of interest." But perhaps another way of understanding it is this: Adam's situation may not impair any decision he takes in role, but it does encumber his decision as to whether to enter his role in the first place—a meta-conflict of interest.[8]

Is Adam in a meta conflict of interest? But first, what is a meta conflict of interest? I venture the following definition: "A meta conflict of interest is a situation in which an interest tempts us to decline to assume an office-, position-, work-, or job-related duty—a situation that threatens the interest of someone else." The thing is, if we decline a position or work, then we will not enter in a conflict of interest, and so no conflict of interest is involved. But even if we admit their existence, they will only occur with potential new clients or principals. If Adam's appointment is with a current client, then we should not speak of a meta conflict of interest. Why? Because attending the client when agreed is an office- or job-related duty. We may even say that meeting the client is, generally speaking, the first duty of a job.

Let's say that Adam is a financial advisor. A current client has some doubts regarding the former and future management of her finances. They arrange a meeting, but when the day arrives Adam feels tempted to go golfing. If he yields to the temptation, he will have failed his client, and thus broken a position- or work-related duty.

INDIVIDUAL AND ORGANIZATIONAL
CONFLICTS OF INTEREST

A somewhat tricky question when classifying conflicts of interest is whether not only individuals but also organizations can face conflicts of interest. The typical and expected answer is "yes!," but the topic is more complex, and the way it is treated in the literature reflects this complexity. Luebke, for instance, openly defends the existence of the *organizational* type:

> Any person or organized group capable of deliberate judgment or action and who acts or is empowered to act in a fiduciary role can have a CI [conflict of interest]. The parties in the fiduciary relationship may be natural persons, partnerships, corporations, nations, voluntary organizations, or political constituencies.[9]

On the other extreme is Carson, who has never straightforwardly argued for the nonexistence of organizational conflicts of interest, but who nevertheless says that "those who have no official duties as employees, professionals in private practice, or members of organisations, cannot have conflicts of interest."[10] In addition, the protagonists of all the examples he presents in his 1994 and 2004 pieces are human beings—never organizations.

Between Luebke and Carson stands Schwab, who begins his paper by saying that all studies on conflicts of interest in recent decades "deal with an individual or organisation pulled in separate directions by their responsibilities and interests."[11] When we keep on reading, though, we find that all the examples he presents are of individuals: not a single one of Schwab's examples has an organization as the protagonist of a conflict of interest.

What is going on? Can organizations, like corporations, have conflicts of interest, like Luebke confidently asserts? Or are organizational conflicts of interest just an illusion? If this is so, then by implication it is individuals in the organization that face them. But how?

I am inclined to say, from a moral (and not a mere legal) perspective, that only "natural" persons can have conflicts of interest. Consider this example.

The A-Team advertising agency. The A-Team advertising agency is an up-and-coming new advertising agency. One of their first and most cherished clients is The Small Bakery, a local store located a few steps away from the agency. Suddenly, though, The A-Team receives an offer from a potential client: Big Bread. Big Bread is a national chain that, like The Small Bakery, sells baked goods. The A-Team accepts the offer without hesitation, only to realize that it now faces a conflict of interest.

Does The A-Team advertising agency face a conflict of interest? It seems so: the company is in a situation in which its interest to make a good impression on Big Bread makes it difficult to properly serve The Small Bakery, endangering the latter's interest. But all this talk feels odd. The A-Team advertising agency has a contractual duty with The Small Bakery, but can we say that it has a *moral* duty to honor it? (More on the moral dimension of work or job duties in the next chapter.) And can the agency be tempted by an interest? Is it the company that is tempted, or its members? It is its members. It is, say, the owners of The A-Team advertising agency who are tempted to favor Big Bread, since this will lead to better profits for the agency and, thus, for them. Or the CEO, if there is one. Or whoever it is in the company who makes the decision and will benefit from it. A company, as an artificial entity, cannot be tempted.

Maybe the above is what moves a scholar like Carson to avoid speaking of organizational conflicts of interest and what (consciously or unconsciously) prevents Schwab from offering examples in which organizations are the protagonists. That said, I am not necessarily suggesting that we stop speaking of organizational conflicts of interest. It may sometimes still be useful to do so (at least, from a legal perspective), but if we look closely at the idea, we cannot help but recognize that it is a problematic one.

ORGANIZATIONAL CONFLICTS OF INTEREST RECONSIDERED

All the same, organizational conflicts of interest deserve a hearing. In his 1992 piece, Boatright devoted some space to defending their existence. He starts with his definition of conflicts of interest, which goes like this:

> A conflict of interest may be described as a conflict that occurs when a personal interest interferes with a person's acting as to promote the interest of another when the person has an obligation to act in that other person's interest. This is equivalent to asserting that a conflict of interest arises when a personal interest interferes in the performance of an agent's obligation to a principal.[12]

After asserting that organizations can face this type of situations as well, Boatright offers a series of iconic examples of organizational conflicts of interest: accounting firms providing lucrative management services to the same companies they audit, investment banking houses financing takeovers of companies with whom they have long-standing relations, law firms accepting clients with competing interests, and so forth. The A-Team advertising agency will, in his opinion, undoubtedly face a conflict of interest.

But would the inclusion of organizations as protagonists of conflicts of interest not affect the definition? Not in his opinion, since:

> [a] organizations as well as individuals can be agents and can have organizational obligations and interests that are not necessarily those of the individuals who compose an organization. [b] The term "person" can simply be expanded in this instance to include organizations without entering into the lively debate over whether organizations are persons.[13]

Let's analyze the assertions here identified as "a" and "b."

With regard to "a"—the assertion that organizations can have organizational obligations and interests that are not necessarily those of the individual who compose an organization—it would definitively have helped if Boatright had explained it in detail. As a matter of fact, this would have addressed the doubts raised in the last section regarding the purported moral obligation of organizations and companies to honor their contractual duties, and the possibility that these same entities might feel tempted by interests. This leads us now to the next, more substantial point.

With regard to "b"—the assertion that we can expand the term "person" in the definition of conflicts of interest "without entering into the lively debate over whether organisations are persons"—well, it is one way of circumventing the problem. The problem of the existence of organizational conflicts of interest, though, cannot be truly solved without determining whether organizations are persons, i.e., entities with moral duties, interests and, thus, moral problems. But do they? Or when we say that an organization has moral duties, interests, and thus conflicts of interest, are we only speaking metaphorically?

We are back to where we were in the last section: to speak of organizational conflicts of interest feels odd. To be more precise, it does not feel odd to speak of organizational conflicts of interest *per se*. To many, it may be the opposite: to deny their existence feels odd. Rather, what is odd is to say that an organization is a sort of living entity that can be tempted to act wrongly, and thus face moral problems such as conflicts of interest. In other words, when we realize what a conflict of interest is, the oddness of speaking of organizational conflicts of interest emerges in full force.

That said, we will not resolve this matter until we settle the very question that Boatright avoids—namely, whether organizations are persons in the full sense of the word.

TEXT BOX 4.3: DO COMPANIES AND ORGANIZATIONS HAVE MORAL RESPONSIBILITIES?

The question of whether companies and organizations in general can face conflicts of interest is part of a bigger one: namely, whether they can have moral (and not only legal) responsibilities. It would take a whole chapter, perhaps even a book, to explain the debate and take a fully informed position. What follows is just a sample.

Consider the question from a Kantian perspective (on which this book is grounded, alongside utilitarianism). When it comes to the moral responsibilities of companies, scholars such as Norman E. Bowie (arguably the most important Kantian business ethicist) have no problem with speaking of corporations as moral agents with moral responsibilities. In fact, Bowie could do this all day long.[14] But what if they are wrong?

Matthew C. Altman argues precisely this in "The Decomposition of the Corporate Body: What Kant Cannot Contribute to Business Ethics":

> A business has neither inclinations nor the capacity to reason, so it lacks the conditions necessary for constraint by the moral law. Instead, corporate policies ought to be understood as analogous to legal constraints. They may encourage or discourage certain actions, but they cannot determine a person's maxims—which for Kant is the focus of moral judgment.[15]

Prima facie, I am with Altman on this one. If an organization cannot distinguish right from wrong and cannot be tempted, how can it have moral responsibilities? I simply cannot see how.

Of course, this does not close the case, since it is possible to argue for the moral responsibilities of organizations from a different, more "collectivistic" perspective. This is what Altman suggests, but I doubt it can work. Answering Altman, though, would mean joining the wider debate in full—and, as I said, this would take a lot of space, but, more importantly, lead us astray.

EXTRINSIC CONFLICTS OF INTEREST

As Stark has taught us, conflicts of interest can also be classified based on the origin of the interest tempting one to disregard the duty. If the tempting interest comes from outside the office, position, work, or job, we are facing an out-of-role or *extrinsic* conflict of interest. If the interest comes from within the job, then we will face an in-role or *intrinsic* conflict of interest.[16]

The "Independent" business consultant. Logan is an independent business consultant. He is currently advising Tom, an old client, on the expansion of his car workshop—a business Logan successfully helped to launch. One day, Logan is visited by a mysterious person. The visitor begins speaking of his own business (also a car workshop), and finally reveals the reason for his visit: Logan should give poor business advice to Tom, so as to secure his failure. In exchange, he will receive enough money to retire—or else.

This is an instance of extrinsic conflict of interest. It is extrinsic since the interest (money and fear) Logan now has in disregarding his position- or job-related duty comes from outside the relationship between Logan and his client, Tom.

If we look closely at the examples used in this and the former chapter, we will realize that most of them are also instances of extrinsic conflicts of interest: the "friendly" human resources executive (interested in getting her friend a job), the general manager in love (interested in securing a contract for his girlfriend), the acquisitive financial adviser (interest in making his family richer), the nationalist financial adviser (interest in serving his country), the broken-hearted photographer (interest in punishing an ex-lover), the resentful dog-walker (interest in punishing a mean dog), the "informal" entrepreneur (interest in getting free meals), and the lovestruck supplier (interest in advancing his sweetheart's business)—all of them faced extrinsic conflicts of interest. Only The A-Team advertising agency and the greedy stockbroker were instances of intrinsic conflicts of interest. How has this happened? Was it on purpose?

I did not do this on purpose. Extrinsic conflicts of interest are very popular—much more popular (but, alas, not more common) than the intrinsic type. In fact, the former are so popular that we tend to overlook the latter's existence. This is a widespread problem. If you open a code of ethics document at random, chances are that you will not find examples of intrinsic conflicts of interest there. I say this is a problem because intrinsic conflicts of interest are not only as common extrinsic ones, but they are as morally problematic as well. And why would not this be the case? Interests come from all places, and when they come they tempt us to disregard an office- or work-related duty.

Something interesting about extrinsic conflicts of interest is that, unlike the intrinsic type (as we will soon see), they are all very similar. As Stark explains:

> A personal gift from an individual external to the professional–principal relationship—a pharmaceutical manufacturer in the case of

the—physician-patient relationship, a mutual fund salesman in the case of the broker–client relationship—impairs the professional's judgment in all three pursuits in exactly identical way. A judge's decision-making is threatened in precisely the same fashion as a journalist's—or a corporate director's—by her capacity to affect an out-of-role financial holding through her in-role decision making.[17]

In this quote, Stark mentions external conflicts of interest that are borne of tangible interests, but the same can be said of conflicts that emerge from intangible interests like love, hate, etcetera (recall, again, our examples). In other words, external intangible interests tempt in exactly the same way the human resource executive, the photographer, the financial analyst, the seller, and so on—thereby creating extrinsic conflicts of interest.

INTRINSIC CONFLICTS OF INTEREST 1: MANY PRINCIPALS, ONE DUTY

If out-of-role or extrinsic conflicts of interest all look alike, in-role or intrinsic conflicts of interest do not. This is where diversity unfolds, and where the classification reaches full fruition. As Stark explains:

Some [conflicts of interest] arise because the professional occupies more than one role with respect to the same principal, such that the existence of the second role impairs her capacity to exercise the first [many roles, one principal]. Others occur because the professional must exercise the same role with respect to more than one principal, such that the presence of a second principal impairs her capacity to exercise her role on behalf of the first [many principals, one role].[18]

To bring this distinction closer to the definition of conflicts of interest defended in this book, we should, rather, speak of *many duties, one principal* and *many principals, one duty*—i.e., I propose to replace the word "role" with "duty." We will focus on the "many principals, one duty" type first.

Let's begin by redoing the case of The A-Team advertising agency and speak instead of an independent advertiser (to avoid the deeper discussion of whether organizations can have conflicts of interest).

The A-mazing advertiser. Thal is an amazing advertiser. In fact, she markets herself as the "A-mazing advertiser." She has an old client, The Small Bakery, but has recently signed a contract with a bigger baking company: Big Bread. One night she comes up with an amazing advertising idea for a bakery, and the conflict appears: To whom should she give the idea? The Small Bakery or Big Bread? She cannot share the idea with both. But whoever gets the idea will doubtlessly benefit—at the other's expense.

Thal is in a conflict of interest, in which an interest tempts her to disregard an office-, position-, work-, or job-related duty—a situation that threatens the interest of someone else. The tempting interest, in this case, could be to favor, for financial reasons, the new bigger client (Big Bread). This comes at the expense of the older and smaller one (The Small Bakery). Or it could be to favor the smaller one, this time out of affection for the longer-established relationship. In any case, by favoring one client she will, to some degree, be dishonoring the duty she has with the other.

What makes this example an instance of the intrinsic type of conflicts of interest? And what makes this example an instance of the many principals, one duty subtype? It is an intrinsic conflict of interest because the tempting interest emerges from within the business relationship. In addition, it is an instance of the many principals, one duty subtype because there are many principals with competing interests and one work- or job-related duty which, in this case, is to advertise.

The many principals, one duty subtype of conflict of interest, then, occurs when one person—an entrepreneur, in our example—has: (a) two or more clients or principals to serve, and (b) one office- or position-related duty. To this, I would add a third condition: (c) a scarce good or resource. Two or more principals and one duty will not necessarily generate a conflict of interest—there has to be a scarce good as well: a product, time, an idea, etcetera. If the good abounds, the conflict of interest will not emerge.

To think of another example, let's remember the greedy stockbroker and imagine that the financial product he has to offer is scarce. He will be naturally tempted to recommend it to the bigger client, but this will be unfair to the small ones who expect the best financial product as well. If the product abounded, though, the greedy stockbroker would have had no problem in offering the product to all his clients, and thus would not have faced a conflict of interest.

TEXT BOX 4.4: SOME CONCERNS ABOUT STARK'S CLASSIFICATION

The "many duties, one principal" subtypes. Stark's classification of conflicts of interest is certainly helpful. There are, though, some details that are not completely clear—at least to me. One is the division of the many duties, one principal type into two (see next section): *diagnosing-service* and *judging-advocating*. I cannot, though, put my finger on what bothers me about this classification. Or maybe I can, but I am not sure if what bothers me is well-grounded. In other words, so far I do not have clear answers to the following questions: Is Stark's classification accurate, i.e., can we neatly distinguish between the two types or are there more than a few blurry cases? Is it complete, or are we missing other combinations? Is it helpful, or can we stop at the many principals, one duty and many duties, one principal level without missing anything substantial?

To the extent that I do not have answers to these questions, I think it is fair to give Stark the benefit of the doubt. There is, though, a related problem that I am more confident about tackling.

One duty, one principal? At the beginning of his chapter, Stark presents the following example of the intrinsic type of conflict of interest: that of a government bureaucrat required to decide on supporting a high tech-subsidy, but whose decision "is affected by her desire to advance through the ranks bureaucratically, shift her career path within the department, and increase her official salary."[19] This is an instance of an intrinsic conflict of interest, but of which type? Stark does not say. The problem is, I cannot place it among the many principals, one duty type or the many duties, one principal type either. So what is going on? In short, this seems to be an instance of a category Stark may be missing: the *one duty, one principal* or *one principal, one duty* type of conflict of interest. Unless, of course, it is me who is missing something.

What do I propose, then? To add the one duty, one principal category—and to further clarify, or skip altogether, the many duties, one principal subtypes.

INTRINSIC CONFLICTS OF INTEREST 2:
MANY DUTIES, ONE PRINCIPAL

The other type of intrinsic conflict of interest (and with this we finish the classification) is the many duties, one principal one. Two duties and one principal, though, are not enough to generate this particular conflict of interest. The duties must be somewhat incompatible—incompatible in the sense that, when combined, they spark an interest that threatens the proper performance of one of the job-related duties and, as always, the interest of the principal.

According to Stark, the many duties, one principal type of intrinsic conflict of interest can, in turn, be divided in two. The first subtype emerges when there is a work- or job-related duty to diagnose problems and another to provide services for the same client or principal.[20]

The "thugbuster" of the year. Karen works for a company devoted to digital security: Thugbusters. Companies are very vulnerable to cyberattacks and Thugbusters offers a solution: diagnose and intervene. The "intervene" stage involves both the provision of digital services and the sale of products. Karen is currently attending a big client and feels the recurrent temptation: to over-diagnose and over-sell. Doing that, after all, has positioned her as the "Thugbuster of the year."

Let's analyze Karen's case, identifying the elements that comprise a conflict of interest. (1) Tempting interest: being rewarded by her employer. (2) Job-related duties: diagnosing and providing digital security services. (3) Interest threatened: the client's finances. As we can see, Karen faces a conflict of interest. What makes it this specific type of conflict of interest is the second element, i.e., the "explosive" mixture of her duties.

As Carson warns, this class of conflicts of interest is very common, not only among the employed, but among the self-employed as well: "plumbers, dentists, exterminators, auto mechanics, electricians, psychologists, appliance repairmen, and many other professionals also occupy the dual role of diagnosing problems and providing services."[21] The list, of course, can go on. Consider the occupations mentioned by Stark: accountants, lawyers, brokers, physicians, corporate directors, consulting engineers, and officials. And so on.

Something interesting regarding this subtype of conflict of interest is this: they are the source of our insecurity when we bring our car to the auto mechanic or visit the dentist. We feel powerless and fear that we will be abused.

The second subtype emerges when there is a position- or work-related duty to judge and another to advocate for the same principal.[22] Stark offers two business-related examples: *the primary-market financial underwriter* and *the show-business agent.*

Primary-market financial service underwriters, for their part, find themselves in a conflict of interest that involves judging and advocacy when they are supposed to both assess and promote a client's initial public offering. In the case of show-business agents, they face conflicts of interest of this class when promoting an actor while, at the same time, producing shows that may not necessarily benefit from the actor's participation.

Here, we find the same elements as before: a tempting interest, two (incompatible) work- or job-related duties (in this case, judging and advocating), and a principal whose interest is threatened.

Of all the types of conflicts of interest in business, this type may be the least common. Why do I think this? Because of the difficulty in finding examples—in the literature and in my mind. The polar opposite is the case of extrinsic conflicts of interest, which are very common and very easy to conceive and identify. But intrinsic conflicts of interest exist, regardless. As such, they deserve consideration.

CHAPTER SUMMARY

In this chapter, I unfolded a comprehensive typology of conflicts of interests. I began with a justification of the classification itself, showing how, like with virtues (and anything), it will give us a better understanding of what conflicts of interest are.

The classification itself began with the distinction between formal and informal conflicts of interest. If conflicts of interest require an office-, position-, work-, or job-related duty, then it follows that only formal conflicts of interest will exist. The fact, though, that not every business, organization, or deal is formal led us to reconsider this and admit the existence of informal conflicts of interest, i.e., of conflicts that involve an informal position- or job-related duty (the "informal" entrepreneur).

I then discussed potential and actual conflicts of interests. A potential conflict of interest is one in which the person facing the conflict (the lovestruck supplier) does not yet have to execute the job-related duty. An actual conflict of interest, on the other hand, is one in which the duty needs to be executed immediately.

Next, I considered apparent conflicts of interest. As the name suggests, these are not real conflicts but they seem real to third parties. Because of this, they are still somewhat problematic. An apparent conflict of interest is merely apparent either because there is either no office- or work-related duty involved (the competitive bull breeder) or no interest threatening the duty (Smith the smith).

Moving on to individual and organizational conflicts of interest, I contemplated whether only natural persons face conflicts of interest or whether artificial ones like businesses, institutions, etcetera do as well. Though it may seem extreme to deny organizational conflicts of interest, I explained how, when considered carefully, it is certainly odd and arbitrary to speak of an organization being tempted by an interest. It is the persons within the organization who feel the temptations, not the artificial entity. To that extent, it may be the case that only individual conflicts of interest exist. The A-Team advertising agency brought this point closer.

Finally, I explored the division between extrinsic and intrinsic conflicts of interest. Conflicts of interest are extrinsic when the tempting interest comes from outside the office, position, work, or job (the "independent" business consultant). These are the most popular—so much so that codes of ethics almost always reduce conflicts of interest to this class.[23] Intrinsic conflicts of interest, on the other hand, occur when the tempting interest comes from inside the job (the A-mazing advertiser).

Intrinsic conflicts of interest, in turn, can be divided into two: the many principals, one duty type; and the many duties, one principal one. The former occurs not only when there are many principals and one duty, but also when there is a scarce resource (the A-mazing advertiser). The latter, in turn, occurs when the duties owed to the principal are somewhat incompatible.

The many duties, one principal type, in turn, can be divided in two as well: the first, when there is a duty to diagnose and another to provide a service ("Thugbuster" of the year); the second, when there is a duty to judge and another to advocate (the primary-market financial underwriter).

In between, I discussed the problem of expanding informal conflicts of interests, meta conflicts of interest, whether companies and organizations can have moral responsibilities, and some problems with Stark's classification.

Now, let's return to the magic trick. My powers only extend so far, so I cannot tell the exact example you were thinking of, but I bet your conflict of interest was of the actual, individual, and extrinsic type. Am I right?

QUESTIONS AND EXERCISES FOR REFLECTION

1. Make a diagram with all the types of conflicts of interest included in this chapter. Add a brief example for each type.
2. Think of a conflict of interest you have personally faced. Why was it a conflict of interest and not just a mere moral problem? And what kind of conflict of interest was it?
3. Open your employer's code of ethics document (or any code of ethics, if you are not currently working) and identify the types of conflicts of interest it regulated. Which types are included? And which are left out?
4. Does the code of ethics include examples? If so, classify the examples.

5. Does the code of ethics you are analyzing include intrinsic conflicts of interest? If so, explain.
6. If you answered "no" to the last question, why do you think this is the case? Why do codes of ethics tend to exclude this whole class of conflicts of interest? Is it just a blind spot or is there something else going on?
7. Do you think it makes sense to speak of organizational conflicts of interest? Or do only individual ones truly exist? Justify your answer.
8. Can you think of a type of conflict of interest not covered in this chapter? If you can, provide an example.
9. How can this classification help you in your professional life?
10. Remember the magic trick. What was your example, and was I right in guessing the type of conflict of interest?

Chapter 5

ASSESSING CONFLICTS
OF INTEREST

Some years ago, a friend told me: "Those who have no conflicts of interests have no interests." I think he meant that conflicts of interests are not problems but healthy signs of an active, interesting, successful life—like the life of Carol.

The super business executive. Carol is in her prime. She has had a remarkably rapid rise at a multinational company and now leads the marketing department. In addition, she manages a popular Instagram account, is a board member of the local chamber of commerce, volunteers for a local charity, has launched a start-up, among other laudable commitments. She can hardly keep track of how her several positions could compromise her objectivity. "It does not matter," she tells herself. "I will never abuse any of my positions and, anyway, what option do I have?"

My friend made me think—doubt, even. Are we (those of us who worry about conflicts of interest) overreacting? Even worse, are we promoting a world of mediocrity—of people who, out of fear and lack of skills, lay to rest their dreams and ambitions, while asking the "Carols" of the world to stop being successful?

This is, perhaps, what Nietzsche, the enemy of traditional morality (that of the moral law), would have said. In *On the Genealogy of Morality* (1887), he argues that ethics is an invention of the weak, or "slaves," to oppress the strong, or "masters." The story goes like this:

Once upon a time, the resentful weak, unable to subject the strong by force, devised a subtle and long-term revolt: to convince them that doing well was, well, not good. The strong (best represented in history by the Romans) had their own way of valuing things. For them, "good" equated to that which characterized them: "good = noble = powerful = beautiful

81

= happy = blessed."[1] "Bad," on the other hand, had no moral connotation, but simply meant "of low quality." The weak were bad in the way a lame horse is.

The weak (best represented in history by the Christians) inverted this mode of valuation and began to brainwash or spiritwash, so to speak, the strong. What the strong regarded as bad began to be regarded as good, and what they regarded as good began to be regarded not merely as bad, but, even worse, as "evil"—bad in a *moral* sense.

"Slave morality" eventually prevailed: Rome itself was converted to it by way of its Christianization. Not only that, but this morality even survived the secularization of the West that began in Modernity. Think of the ethics of Kant and Mill. What are they if not secular ways of presenting Christian ethics? Because, did Jesus not teach to respect individuals and to help those who suffer?

Besides its dark origins, Nietzsche thinks that slave morality weakens us. It does so by teaching us to despise strength, wealth, health, and so on—the very things that the strong used to value. Slave morality, in this way, prevents the emergence of great individuals. Now, Nietzsche does not believe that we should return to "master morality." Rather, he thinks that we must aim to transcend both moralities and create, each one of us, our own (become a "Superman" [*Übermensh*] or, at least, not prevent its emergence through things like participation trophies).

Now, what does all this have to do with conflicts of interest? Going back to what my friend said, the ethics of conflicts of interest would be, under a Nietzschean lens, an extension of slave morality, something that harms humanity by preventing the emergence of great businesspeople and professionals—people like Carol.

Without denying that there is a grain or more of truth in Nietzsche's philosophy (traditional morality, poorly understood, can level us down), I stick to what I espoused in chapter 1: ethics has a noble origin and is a positive force. If this is the case, then conflicts of interest are morally problematic. But why exactly?

A PRELIMINARY NOTE: IS BEING IN A CONFLICT OF INTEREST WRONG IN ITSELF?

We ought to clarify this once and for all: being in a conflict of interest is not wrong in itself. After all, we can face one without it being our fault and even against our will. Even more importantly, we can face a conflict of interest and manage it ethically. Like ordinary moral problems, what ulti-mately matters is how we manage the morally problematic situation. Let's return to the first example of a conflict of interest we used in this book.

The "friendly" human resources executive. Jane is a human resources executive. A position in the company has been opened, and she has been charged with filling it. The deadline is approaching and several competitive candidates are applying, when something unexpected happens. Kate, her best friend, is applying too. Kate knows that she is putting Jane in trouble, but that does not make things any easier for Jane. Now Jane wonders if she should favor Kate at the expense of more qualified individuals.

Jane is in a conflict of interest. She has a duty to hire the best candi-date. If she hires her friend, she will break this duty. So far, though, she has not done anything beyond feeling inclined to act. The same can be said of all the other examples used so far in this book: the general man-ager in love, the greedy stockbroker, the acquisitive financial analyst, the nationalist financial analyst, the broken-hearted photographer, the resent-ful dog walker, the "informal" entrepreneur, the lovestruck supplier, the A-Team advertising agency (if organizational conflicts of interests exist), the "independent" business consultant, the A-mazing advertiser, and the "Thugbuster" of the year. They were all inclined to break their job duties, and thus act immorally, but had not done so yet.

We need, then, to distinguish between being tempted to do some-thing wrong and actually doing so. The former is problematic; the second, condemnable. It goes without saying that our proneness to be tempted is something not to be taken lightly. If we find ourselves tempted all the time by all sorts of things, we have moral homework to do. What kind of homework? Virtue-related homework (recall last chapter's introduction).

The idea that being in a conflict of interest is not wrong in itself does not imply, to be sure, that it is morally acceptable to put oneself in a conflict of interest or that we should not take care to avoid them. Putting oneself in a conflict of interest is morally wrong just like putting oneself in an ordinary moral problem is. Why is it wrong? Because we cannot know, in advance, how we are going to manage the problem. When we put ourselves in a conflict of interest we add moral risk to our lives, thus increasing the chances of acting immorally. It is like the married person who joins dating apps, the recovering alcoholic who stores away some booze "just in case," or the spendthrift who accepts yet another credit card.

In the case of Jane the HR executive, this would have been the case, for instance, if she had commented the open position to Kate, in the hope that her friend would apply and they could spend more time together.

Jane can, it is true, ultimately hire the best candidate, but there is no guarantee that she will do so. Had she, instead, not pursued the conflict of interest, she would have made her life, morally speaking, easier. Yes, conflicts of interests must be evaded when possible for the reasons we are going to discuss very soon.

With this talk of evading conflicts of interest, though, we are entering the realm of their management, which is the next chapter's topic. Suffice to say for now that being in a conflict of interest is not wrong in itself, but it is morally problematic. This insight is important to the extent that we can rush and condemn someone for being in a conflict of interest when that person is not responsible for being in one. In other words, we can commit an injustice.

TEXT BOX 5.1: REMEMBERING KANT'S DEONTOLOGY AND MILL'S UTILITARIANISM

We will now speak again of the moral law and the secondary duties it begets. In other words, we will apply more intensively the moral theories we outlined and discussed in chapter 1: Kant's deontology and Mill's utilitarianism. This invites a short reminder of the central tenets of both theories.

Kant's deontology. According to Kant, reason orients us in life. And it not only orients us strategically—it orients us morally as well. In other words, reason is the source of a moral law that commands, categorically, to live in a certain way. Which way? According to maxims or personal principles that we can will to become universal laws. If we cannot will the universalization of the maxims that orient us in life, then the maxims, and the actions they inspire, are immoral. This insight opens the door to another one: the idea of humans as ends in themselves, i.e., as beings with dignity. Thus, the alternative formulation of the same moral law: that which commands to never treat humans as mere means (this since we are moral beings, capable of distinguishing right from wrong and to do what is right, i.e., to act autonomously).

Mill's utilitarianism. Mill believes in a moral law as well, but this law would order something different. It would order, in its most famous formulation, to promote the greatest happiness for the greatest amount of people. And what is happiness? Pleasure and the absence of pain—corporeal and mental or spiritual. Thus, the moral law would order to promote the greatest amount of pleasure (or, at least, to reduce the greatest amount of pain) for the greatest number of people. But why? What are the grounds for this version of the moral law? Happiness or pleasure itself, says Mill. In other words, assuming that happiness is the only thing we desire as an end, it would follow that it is the highest good that we must all promote—and not only for our own selves, but for as many other people as possible.

JOB-RELATED DUTIES AS "TERTIARY" DUTIES OF MORALITY

But why exactly are conflicts of interest moral problems instead of, say, just labor, contractual, or legal ones? After all, the duties at stake in them do not look like moral ones. Or would you say that the duties of selling software, managing a division, or securing a supplier are ordinary moral duties, i.e. duties that all humans have by virtue of being humans? No, these duties only apply to sellers, managers, and supply chain specialists, respectively. But if these duties have no moral dimension, then we should stop treating conflicts of interest as moral problems. Something is missing. First, we must see that job-related duties spring from promises. As Carson notes:

> A person's official duties aren't necessarily moral duties, even *prima facie* moral duties [a duty that one recognizes at first glance, but that can be overturn with a strong reason]. However, ordinarily, one has a contractual or promissory (moral) duty to fulfil the duties of one's office or position. Offices within organizations and relationships between professionals and their clients carry with them special duties. A person who voluntarily assumes an office within an organization (or a professional who voluntarily takes on a client) tacitly agrees or promises to fulfil those duties. Ordinarily, these agreements create at least a *prima facie* moral obligation to fulfil the duties in question.[2]

Second, we must recognize that keeping our promises is a moral duty. Carson calls this duty a prima facie one, but we might also call it a secondary duty of morality.

Remember that, in chapter 2, we talked of the moral law as our primary duty and of the secondary duties it produces. This view of the moral law as producing secondary duties was one of those things on which both Kant and Mill agreed. Now, among these duties there is that of keeping promises. But if this is indeed the case (if there is such a duty, as common sense dictates and as I will develop in the following sections), it would be a moral duty to honor work-related duties. Why? Because, as mentioned, they spring from promises—the promises we make when accepting offices, positions, works, or jobs.

Job-related duties are like the adopted children of the moral duty to keep promises. Like the latter, they are duties, but not inherently moral ones—it is a promise, not a moral duty, that begets them. Now, given that the promise will not, by itself, be able to keep its offspring in good shape, the duty to keep promises steps up and takes them under its wing. In this way, job-related duties join the family of moral duties. From this perspective, if the duty to keep promises is a secondary duty of morality, position- or job-related duties would be tertiary duties of morality—even if not by birth.

Another way of putting it is to say that the secondary duty of keeping promises is a duty that gains further content, or gets further specified, with promises. The moral law produces the duty of keeping promises, but promises have content. Because of this, the duty to keep promises can be completed or rephrased in each specific case with the content of the office-, position-, work-, or job-related promise.

For instance, imagine I promise to manage a company. The general moral duty of keeping promises, in my particular case, can be rephrased as the duty to keep my promise to manage a company. Work- or job-related duties, under this light, are nothing but the duty of keeping promises "incarnated" in office, position, work, or job-related contexts.

If I do not manage the company properly, but use the position to benefit myself, my family, and friends, I will be dishonoring my duty to do so. Now, dishonoring this duty, in turn, implies breaking the duty to keep promises. Breaking the duty to keep promises, ultimately, implies breaking the moral law. But why is keeping promises a moral duty? How it is derived from the moral law? Let's explore these questions further.

BREAKING PROMISES: A DEONTOLOGICAL ANALYSIS 1

Let's think through why breaking promises is immoral and, thus, why it is a moral duty to keep them—starting with Kant. Actually, we have already talked about promises in the Kantian context: in chapter 1 we derived the duty to not make lying promises from the moral law in the formula of universal law. We used an example from the financial world: a person in financial stress requesting a loan.

An almost identical analysis can be done with the sister duty of not breaking truthful promises, so let's do exactly that. Let's also keep the example, but switch to the other side of the table: that of the lender.

The "friendly" financial agent. Margot works for a bank. She is in charge of approving loans. A file just arrived with her best friend's name on it. It is Claudia, who, despite being on the verge of losing her job (as she told Margot last weekend), has asked for a loan as if she were in a stable position. Margot knows Claudia made a false promise about her ability to repay the loan when she requested it. Because of their friendship, though, Margot feels inclined to turn a blind eye and approve the request—despite wondering if it would be ethical to do so.

Claudia is acting immorally, but does not face a conflict of interest—Margot does. Margot is in a situation in which an intangible interest (a friendship) tempts her to disregard a job-related duty—a situation that threatens the interest of her employer. If she yields to the interest, she will break her duty to approve loans objectively, and will in turn break the truthful promise she made to her employer when she was hired.

Now recall the formula of Kant's universal law: "Act only according to that maxim whereby you can at the same time will that it should become a universal law."[3] Recall, as well, the three steps: identify the maxim, paraphrase it as a universal law, and ask yourself if you could coherently support both. Here we go.

The maxim goes something like this: "Whenever it is in my interest, I will break the promise I made to my employer when accepting my job—like the one to approve loans appropriately." The universalized version of the maxim, in turn, would be: "Whenever it is in their interest, workers will break the promises they made to their employers when accepting a job." Now for the analysis. Can anyone coherently support both the maxim and the universalized version? No; it is impossible. If one wills to break a promise when convenient, one cannot (coherently) will a universal law of promise breaking. Why? Because if promise breaking became universal, nobody would believe in promises and they, along with jobs, would disappear. To will the maxim's universalized version is to will the end of promises and jobs, and thus the end of the maxim. To put this in reverse, to will the maxim is to will promises and jobs and thus not the maxim's universalized version. Now, since it is impossible to will the maxim and its universalized version, the maxim is immoral.

Like anyone in her position, Margot the bank clerk wills the opposite of the maxim—namely, promise keeping—but considers making an arbitrary exception in her (and her friend's) favor. She considers playing dirty, breaking rules that she otherwise supports. This explains why breaking promises is immoral, which, in turn, affirms the moral duty of keeping promises.

Focusing on duty, its derivation can be summarized as follows:

1. It is a moral duty to act with maxims that we would universalize.
2. Promise breakers cannot will the universalization of their maxim.
∴ It is a moral duty to keep promises.

Premise 1 contains the moral law in the formula of universal law. Premise 2 expresses another fact: the impossibility of willing the universalization of an immoral maxim. If premises 1 and 2 are true, then the duty to keep promises necessarily follows.

TEXT BOX 5.2: THE FORMULA OF HUMANITY: COMMON MISTAKES

Kant's moral law in the formula of humanity (to be used next) orders to treat humanity always as an end and never simply as a means. A light or superficial reading of this formula can lead to some interpretative mistakes. You need not commit them, though, since here they are listed and clarified.

Mistake 1: "According to Kant, as long as you never treat others never simply as a means (i.e., with respect), you can do whatever you want." Wrong. When reading the formula carefully, it commands to treat yourself with respect as well. Because, yes, we can treat our own selves disrespectfully. The example Kant presents is suicide, which implies "making use of his person merely as a means."[4]

Mistake 2: "According to Kant, you can never treat any person as a means." Wrong. This would make human life impossible. We serve others and people serve us all the time: at the market, at the hair salon, and so forth. The problem lies not in treating persons as a means, but in treating persons *simply* as a means. Thus, when someone serves someone, the latter must treat the former with respect: by recognizing his or her humanity.

Mistake 3: "Kant's ethics is minimalistic: it sets up some ethical minimums (do not kill, do not steal, etcetera), but nothing beyond that." Wrong. Kant's ethics is very demanding. It not only demands that we never treat humans simply as a means, but that we treat humans as ends at the same time. This explains the meritorious duties of developing our talents and helping the needy that Kant also derives from the moral law.[5]

I mentioned consent as not being enough in ethics. This is an important remark during times where ethics tends to be reduced by many to consent. Now consider the many things we can consent to that clearly would denigrate us: being eaten by another human for pleasure,[6] being hired to fight a war,[7] or being tattooed with brands for money.[8]

BREAKING PROMISES: A DEONTOLOGICAL ANALYSIS 2

Now let's derive the duty to not break promises from the moral law in the formula of humanity. And let's use a different example.

The "loyal" director. Kenneth is a member of the board of directors of a corporation. He was proposed by the CEO almost a year ago. The year is ending and, with it, his term as a board member. The CEO has lately made very questionable business decisions and the board is supposed to ratify or rectify them. Kenneth does not have a single doubt that the CEO needs to be put under scrutiny, but hesitates. After all, the CEO has asked him to stay on the board for another year. "I owe him loyalty," he tells himself.

Kenneth is in a conflict of interest. The interests of prestige and money tempt him to overlook the CEO's questionable management. If he does overlook this, he will be breaking the promise he made to the shareholders when he accepted his position. The question, again, is: Why would it be wrong to yield to his interests—why is breaking promises wrong, this time according to the moral law in the formula of humanity?

Recall the formula of humanity: "Act in such a way that you treat humanity, whether in your own person or in the person of another, always at the same time as an end and never simply as a means."[9] (Recall, as well, how this formula is linked to that of universal law: if it is true that there is a moral law that commands to act on universalizable maxims, we are moral beings and thus ends worthy of respect).

Let's look back at the example through the prism of Kant: intending to break a promise, the "loyal" director will immediately see that he intends to make use of the shareholders as a means to an end that the latter do not likewise hold. The end is to keep his position on the board for his own sake, instead of for the sake of the corporation. Can the shareholders hold the end of his action? Impossible, since this would jeopardize the future of the corporation.

One may ask: do all board members (and workers) not use share-holders merely as a means to an end—as a means to money? And do all shareholders not use board members (and workers) the same way—merely as a means to profit? Not necessarily. We are social beings and, because of that, we cannot avoid using each other as means. Life would be impossible otherwise. The challenge is to not treat each other *simply* as means, always recognizing each other's humanity.

Back to Kenneth; what he is considering doing is disrespectful. He wants to remain a board member, but instead of doing what they should be doing—serving shareholders—he considers serving himself by helping the CEO. The shareholders, though, would never have accepted Kenneth's position as a board member if they had known this.

If we outline (as we did with the formula of universal law) the derivation of the duty to keep promises from the formula of humanity, it looks as follows:

1. It is a moral duty to never treat humanity simply as a means.
2. Promise breakers treat others merely as a means.
∴ It is a moral duty to keep promises.

Premise 1 contains the moral law in the formula of humanity. Premise 2 expresses another fact: promise breakers do not recognize the humanity of others. If premises 1 and 2 are true, then the duty of keeping promises follows.

Summarizing the Kantian analysis, there is a duty to keep promises to the extent that there is a higher duty to act on universalizable maxims and to treat humanity always as an end. Promise breakers will never support the universalization of their maxims. When they break promises, they further treat others simply as means—bypassing the fact that they are ends, beings with dignity who, because of that, deserve respect.

BREAKING PROMISES: A UTILITARIAN ANALYSIS 1

Let's now analyze promise breaking from the utilitarian perspective. Here, distinguishing between two types of utilitarianism will allow us to carry out a more comprehensive evaluation; I refer to act and rule utilitarianism.

According to act utilitarianism, an action is right if it promotes general happiness. Thus, if I consider breaking a promise and doubt if it would be ethical to do so, I am called upon to evaluate whether doing so in this specific situation would, all things considered, promote or hamper general happiness.

According to rule utilitarianism, on the other hand, an action is right if it accords with a rule that tends to promote general happiness. Thus, if I consider breaking a promise and doubt if it is ethical to do so, I am called upon to ponder whether a rule that allows promise breaking would favor or inhibit general happiness.

Experts debate what kind of utilitarianism Mill defended.[10] In chapter 1, I took a position without making it explicit—I showed by explanation that Mill is a rule utilitarian. When, exactly, does he demonstrate this, you may wonder? When answering whether utilitarianism requires that we calculate the consequences of everything we do at all times. Mill's answer is that we do not. We do not because we (all of us) have inherited a moral code, made up of basic rules of conduct, that tend to promote general happiness. This code, Mill goes on to argue, is not arbitrary but the result of thousands of years of experience—experience that teaches us that there are certain things, like murder, that hurt society's well-being, and others, like charity, that promote it. Mill invites us to trust this moral code, albeit not dogmatically. Indeed, Mill invites us to improve it when necessary and is open to rule breaking in extreme cases. Both, though, should be done very exceptionally and after careful utilitarian consideration. In these matters, it is unwise to rush.

We do not have to establish whether Mill was an act or rule utilitarian for our purposes, however. We can instead show that, in both cases, utilitarianism will favor promise keeping—beginning with act utilitarianism.

Performing act utilitarianism requires, by definition, evaluating cases one by one. Consider the case of Margot, the "friendly" financial agent, again. What would happen if she yielded to the temptation to give the loan to her (financially problematic) friend? What would happen, in other words, if she broke the promise she made to her employers to assign loans properly? I can think of the following outcomes.

First, her employers will suffer financial loss. Had they given the loan to a truthful lender, they would have earned the corresponding interest. Add the risk of not even recovering all of their money and the financial loss increases. Second, they will have to resort to legal procedures to recover their money—wasting more money and, in addition, time. Third, they will trust less in their workers and, perhaps, in society in general. Fourth, because of this increased distrust, they will probably implement more policies and regulations to prevent this from happening again. But things in the company will become more bureaucratic, which will lead to more time and money wasted for everyone who deals with the bank. Fifth, the bank itself will be less profitable, which will lead to losses on the part of their clients. And so on and so forth. Most ironically, Margot's friend will most probably also end up worse off than she was to begin with. Banks are powerful and will go after her with everything they have. Had Margot kept her promise, none of this would have happened.

This is just a rough analysis of a single case. In all likelihood, if you apply this analysis to the other cases presented in this book, the conclusion will be the same: except very exceptionally, every broken promise (and thus every mismanaged conflict of interest) leaves things worse than they were.

TEXT BOX 5.3: UTILITARIANISM: COMMON MISTAKES

If Kant's formula of humanity can lead to misunderstandings and objections, so too can Mill's utilitarianism. In chapter 1, we dealt with some. Here are some other objections Mill answered in his *Utilitarianism*.

Objection 1: "Utilitarianism does not work in practice." Wrong. To show how this is the case Mill points out the main sources of human suffering: selfishness, want of mental cultivation, and calamities. On the first two, Mill highlights how humans are not fated to be either selfish or uncultivated. On the latter, he argues that, due to human progress, these calamities will affect us less and less. Thus, "all the grand sources . . . of human suffering are in a great degree . . . conquerable."[11]

Objection 2: Utilitarianism promotes selfishness. The answer to this should be obvious at this point, but this misperception is not uncommon among those who, unlike us, have not had the luck of being introduced to the utilitarian principle. In response, Mill says "As between his own happiness and that of others, utilitarianism requires him to be as strictly impartial as a disinterested and benevolent spectator."[12] From this perspective, utilitarianism will eventually demand our sacrifice for the sake of general happiness.

Objection 3: Utilitarianism demands too much from us. This is the opposite of the former objection. But is it true? Mill here lowers the moral bar by claiming two things. First, that for utilitarianism, an action's rightness is not affected by the intention behind it, i.e., by whether it was motivated by duty. Second, that the happiness that one is supposed to promote is limited by one's power. Ordinarily, utilitarianism demands that we only promote the happiness of "some few persons."[13]

The latter thesis invites a further reflection: nowadays, due in great part to technology, regular people can make a much bigger difference than was possible in Mill's times. This is the core message of the (utilitarian-inspired) movement-effective altruism.[14]

BREAKING PROMISES: A UTILITARIAN ANALYSIS 2

With act utilitarianism, we can define if a particular act is immoral as follows:

1. It is a moral duty to promote general happiness.
2. Promise breaking in this particular case will hurt general happiness.
∴ It is a moral duty not to break a promise in this particular case.

Premise 1 contains the principle of utility, the validity of which we discussed in chapter 1. Premise 2 is a case-by-case analysis, like the one we just performed with the "friendly" financial agent. If both premises are true, then the conclusion necessarily follows and we should avoid breaking the promise—in this particular case.

What we ultimately want, though, is to derive a rule or secondary duty that forbids promise breaking in general. In this, rule utilitarianism serves us better and the argument has to be reformulated as follows:

1. It is a moral duty to promote general happiness.
2. Promise breaking tends to hurt general happiness.
∴ It is a moral duty to keep promises.

Like with act utilitarianism, the natural thing to do—assuming that the principle of utility is real—is to empirically prove Premise 2. Considering Mill's speech on the origin of the universal moral code of humanity, though, we could go straight to the conclusion—by recognizing that the rule of promise keeping belongs to this code.

And doesn't it? Is it not a rule you have heard of countless times—a rule that your parents, your teachers, and society in general taught you when you were a child, regardless of where you come from. Do you still doubt it? Then try this: ask yourself if the criminal code of your country punishes fraud. If so, as I am sure is the case, then your society certainly recognizes the duty to keep promises, since fraud frequently involves broken promises. You may want to contest the soundness of the rule (perhaps you are a nihilist or suchlike), but the point here is to recognize that the rule belongs to traditional morality virtually everywhere.[15]

If the rule belongs to this moral code, as indeed it does, then according to Mill's argument there is a strong presumption that it promotes general happiness. Why? Because, to make it into the code, the rule must have passed a rigorous test—the test of consequences throughout history. Of course, skipping Premise 2 in this way sounds somewhat dogmatic, but if we want we can prove the validity of the premise by, well, reviewing history and emblematic cases of broken promises.

Consider recent history. Does the name Bernie Maddof sound familiar? What about Enron? The Great Recession itself was the culmination of a series of broken promises that sent the world into a massive crisis: the promises of financial agents, accreditors, politicians, and others besides—all of whom served themselves instead of doing what they were meant to do when they took their jobs. The rule utilitarism argument can thus be expanded as follows:

1. It is a moral duty to promote general happiness.
2. Promise breaking hurt general happiness in Case 1.
3. Promise breaking hurt general happiness in Case 2.
[. . .]
1000. Promise breaking hurt general happiness in Case 999.
x: Promise breaking hurt general happiness in Case x-1.
∴ Promise breaking tends to hurt general happiness.
∴ It is a moral duty to keep promises.

TAKING CARE OF WHAT WE ARE RESPONSIBLE FOR

As we can see, under both Kant's deontology and Mill's utilitarianism promises (and, thus, work-related duties) must be honored. Speaking of consequences, consider the following.

Each of us is in charge of a small parcel of the world. We occupy a certain position, are in charge of a certain job, and offer something to the world. It does no matter how important we are—whether we are the CEO of a multinational or a clerk who moves documents from office to office. I bet that, if you think it through, what you are doing is much more important to the world than what you think.

The disgruntled secretary. Mario is a secretary at a local company. These are some of his work-related duties: sorting mail, filing, answering phones, scheduling meetings, and so on. His disillusionment makes him mad with his employer and he wants to see the company go under. This moves him to do everything the wrong way—leaving, of course, no trace. By spoiling a merely formal work (burying mail, mixing up files, etc.), he gradually sends the company to the abyss. "Who cares?" he says to himself. "What I do has no relevance."

I have not established what kind of company Mario works for, and this is intentional. Imagine it is an apparently irrelevant, outmoded company—a company like Dunder Mifflin Paper Company (from the U.S. version of the TV show *The Office*).[16] Broadly speaking, because of the mismanagement, its clients will not receive their products on time, or will receive something other than what they ordered, etcetera. This in turn will affect their own mission—at least until they get a new supplier. Now, Dunder Mifflin Paper Company has all sorts of clients, some doing more important things than others, so the consequences of that delay multiply and can eventually become serious.

Imagine a small town with a judge pressed to issue a search warrant that might lead to the arrest of a dangerous criminal. Or a police department seeking to post the image of a missing child around the town soon after the disappearance. Now imagine a local government looking to enforce the temporary closure of a restaurant because of serious security concerns. Without the piece of paper, the criminal could escape, the child could be lost forever, and the restaurant could go on fire while serving diners. Keep imagining the many other important things that are still done with paper: marriages, contracts, passports, etcetera. We may reasonably wish, for ecological purposes, the disappearances of paper, but it is still being used and, for a handful of things at least, we may always need it.

If we extend our glance to the consequences for Dunder Mifflin Paper Company, its shareholders, workers, and families, it is clear that the damage the disgruntled secretary could cause is even worse. Things will be much worse, of course, if we are not talking of Dunder Mifflin Paper Company but of, say, Facebook.

This speaks of the need to have a clear idea of what we (each of us) do for a living and what difference it makes. What would happen if we did our job poorly? Moreover, what would happen if everyone in our role performed poorly? What kind of chaos would ensue? You may be surprised about what you find. For instance, you may find that what you do is objectively more important that what the CEO does. Are you a plumber for a building company? The guy who mops the floor at a clinic? Things could get really bad if you do not take your job seriously.

The disgruntled secretary—and anyone unhappy at work—should not undermine his employer. Doing so is not only (primarily?) disrespectful, but most probably will also lead to serious consequences, as this section has attempted to make clear. Instead, the disgruntled secretary should make a sound plan to change his job as soon as life allows.

TEXT BOX 5.4: CONFLICTS OF INTEREST, BRIBES, AND CORRUPTION

This focus on the consequences of mismanaged conflicts of interest invites a discussion of conflicts of interest, bribes, and corruption. In short, bribe offers by private parties to public officials tend to create conflicts of interest. If the bribe is compelling enough, the conflict of interest will be mismanaged and corruption will ensue. But what are the consequences of corruption? Let the World Bank explain this for us:

> Corruption has a disproportionate impact on the poor and most vulnerable. . . . Think, for example, of the effect of counterfeit drugs or vaccinations on the health outcomes of children and the life-long impacts that may have on them.
>
> Empirical studies have shown that the poor pay the highest percentage of their income in bribes. For example, in Paraguay, the poor pay 12.6 percent of their income to bribes while high-income households pay 6.4 percent. . . . Every stolen dollar, euro, peso, yuan, rupee, or ruble robs the poor of an equal opportunity in life.
>
> Corruption erodes trust in government and undermines the social contract. This is cause for concern across the globe, but particularly in contexts of fragility and violence, as corruption fuels and perpetuates the inequalities and discontent that lead to fragility, violent extremism, and conflict.
>
> Corruption impedes investment, with consequent effects on growth and jobs. Countries capable of confronting corruption use their human and financial resources more efficiently, attract more investment, and grow more rapidly.[17]

In short, corruption has very negative material and immaterial consequences—a further reason to treat conflicts of interest seriously.

OTHER REASONS THAT EXPLAIN
THEIR PROBLEMATIC NATURE

As discussed, conflicts of interest are morally problematic since they tempt us to break promises—the promise we made when accepting an office, position, work, or job. Promise breaking, in turn, is both disrespectful and tends to lead to bad consequences. These are not, though, the only reasons for seeing them as morally problematic.

Carson signals two problems besides promise breaking: harm to others and deception.[18] More precisely, conflicts of interest risk harm to those we promise something and many times lead to deceiving these same people.

On harm to others, Carson distinguishes this problem from breaking promises, but the way we have considered the latter makes the distinction redundant: breaking promises is ultimately wrong, in part, because of the harm it causes (the bad consequences it brings about).

On deception, it is true: conflicts of interest, when mismanaged, not only involve breaking a promise, but often deception as well. This is so because, to self-serve at the expense of others I will probably need to lie to my employer, client, and others. Recall both the "friendly" financial agent and the disgruntled secretary. In the former case, in order to go ahead with the loan, Margot will (most probably) eventually have to lie about her knowledge of her friend Claudia's work and financial situation. In the latter case, when things start to fall apart, Mario will have to lie regarding his culpability in, say, the misplaced file or the canceled meeting.

Now, mismanaged conflicts of interest may sometimes lead to deception, but they always involve the breaking of a promise. This is another reason to consider this problem as the core one at play in conflicts of interest.

Let's now take a look at what the other experts of conflicts of interest (the same people who helped us with the definition) have to say regarding their morally problematic nature.

In the case of Davis, he sees three problems. First, negligence. This would apply if I found myself in a conflict of interest and did nothing. This would not be out of a will to take advantage of the situation, but out of overconfidence in my ability to do the job to the usual standard. The fact is that we are weaker than we think, and most probably will deliver something of lower quality. In other words, most probably we will self-serve. Second, betrayal of trust through deception. We have already talked about deception, but Davis adds something else: if we in fact deceive our employer, boss, etcetera we will betray the trust they put in us. And this is immoral. Finally, harm to the reputation of the profession, occupation, avocation, or individual in question.[19] This happens even if I report the conflict of interest. How? Because of my diminished reliability.

Luebke, in turn, highlights a single central problem—one already mentioned by Davis. He thinks that the main problem with conflicts of interest is the betrayal of trust that they pose. As he puts it, they risk "destruction of the fiduciary relationship and of the milieu of other current and future fiduciary relationships."[20]

Boatright, finally, besides deception (a problem that he also links to conflicts of interest) mentions the following two problems. First, conflicts of interest risk the failure of fulfillment of an obligation—a freely accepted obligation. Second, diminished service. This occurs even if the service is delivered properly. The diminishment is reflected in the reasonable suspicion that the service could have been better if there was no conflict of interest.[21]

As we can see, conflicts of interest are morally problematic for a series of reasons.

CHAPTER SUMMARY

In this chapter, I answered the question of why conflicts of interests are morally problematic. I began by clarifying how being in one is not wrong in itself. It is not, since often they are unavoidable. The "friendly" human resources executive illustrated this well. This insight came with a warning: putting oneself in one or being careless regarding their avoidance carries moral responsibility.

Next, I explained the moral dimension of conflicts of interest. The element of doubt arises when we realize that the duties at stake therein are office- or work-related duties, instead of ordinary ones like "do not steal" and "do not lie." With regard to this, I proposed that work-related duties are like the "adopted children" of the moral duty to keep promises. In short, these duties originate from promises, and promises must be honored.

From here I argued, from a deontological and a utilitarian perspective, why we must keep our promises, i.e., why this follows from the moral law, and outlined these arguments as follows:

Kantian derivation 1, formula of universal law:

1. It is a moral duty to act with maxims that we would universalize.
2. Promise breakers cannot will the universalization of their maxim.
∴ It is a moral duty to keep promises.

Kantian derivation 2, formula of humanity:

1. It is a moral duty to never treat humanity simply as a means.
2. Promise breakers treat others merely as a means.
∴ It is a moral duty to keep promises.

Utilitarian derivation 1, act utilitarianism:

1. It is a moral duty to promote general happiness.
2. Promise breaking in this particular case will hurt general happiness.
∴ It is a moral duty not to break a promise in this particular case.

Utilitarian derivation 2, rule utilitarianism (short version):

1. It is a moral duty to promote general happiness.
2. Promise breaking tends to hurt general happiness.
∴ It is a moral duty to keep promises.

From here, I made an invitation to reflect on and take stock of the importance of what do we do for a living (or freely for a cause, we should add). The chapter highlighted how even the most seemingly inconsequential positions are important and can harm society if not taken seriously. The disgruntled secretary showed how this is the case.

I finally brought to the table other reasons for taking conflicts of interest seriously: harm to others, deception, negligence, betrayal of trust, harm to the reputation of the profession, failure to fulfill an obligation, and diminished service.

In the midst of all this, I summarized the core of deontology and utilitarianism, addressed common misunderstandings and objections presented against these theories, and discussed how conflicts of interest relate to bribes and corruption.

"Those who have no conflicts of interests have no interests," said my friend, suggesting that conflicts of interest are not morally problematic—or not problematic enough to worry about. The fact is that—as this chapter has shown—conflicts of interest are serious and should be managed wisely. And it is precisely their management that we will discuss in the next chapter.

QUESTIONS AND EXERCISES FOR REFLECTION

1. When exposed to Nietzsche's philosophy, many are seduced. But would it be possible to build an ethics of conflicts of interest from such a critical perspective?
2. Think of the last conflict of interest you were involved in. Were you involved through no fault of your own? Or were you responsible for it to some degree?
3. What is the moral dimension of job-related duties? If you currently work or have worked before, mention, in your answer, one of your job-related duties. If you have not yet worked, think of a typical job-related duty linked to your future profession.
4. Why is breaking promises immoral, according to Kant's version of the moral law in the formula of universal law? Include, in your answer, what this formula commands.
5. Why is breaking promises immoral, according to Kant's version of the moral law in the formula of humanity? Include, in your answer, what this formula commands.
6. What is the difference between act and rule utilitarianism?
7. Why is breaking promises immoral, according to rule utilitarianism?
8. Think of your current or a former job. What were you responsible for? And what would have happened if you did a bad job, i.e., if you self-served at the expense of your work-related duty? If you have not worked yet, use your imagination.
9. Considering this chapter's analysis, why are conflicts of interest morally problematic? What is the main reason given in this chapter?
10. Can you give another reason why conflicts of interest are morally problematic (beyond those offered by Carson, Davis, Luebke, and Boatright)?

Chapter 6

MANAGING CONFLICTS OF INTEREST

So far we have discussed (among other things) what a conflict of interest is, how are they classified, and why are they morally problematic. If you consider yourself a *doer*, you may have been waiting impatiently for this chapter.

Not all the authors who have written on conflicts of interest, in essence, speak of their management; it is mainly Davis, Luebke, Boatright, and Carson that say substantial things about it. Thus, they will be our main interlocutors.

In the case of Davis, Luebke, and MacDonald, they focus on individual or (as Wayne Norman and Chris Macdonald call it) microlevel management and ponder the options a person has when facing a conflict of this sort. Boatright also mentions actions at the individual level (How could one not when speaking of their management?), but speaks of management at the organizational level or mid-level as well. Boatright does not divide the solutions or strategies in this way, but the division is not difficult to do.

The present chapter organizes, expands, and reflects upon these proposals. The first five sections are devoted to the (herein titled) five "E"s of individual management (of conflicts of interest): *explore, evade, escape, expose,* and *execute.* The last three sections, in turn, are devoted to the (herein titled as well) ABC of organizational management: *align, build walls,* and *codify.* These principles are called "organizational" since they can only be implemented by organizations (that is, an employee cannot impose regulations through a code of ethics upon his or her employer).

I referred to Boatright as the champion of organizational management. He also presents a strategy at the macrolevel: *competition.* He says: "Strong competition provides a powerful incentive to avoid conflicts of interest. . . .

Insofar as conflicts of interest make organisations less efficient, they pay a price in the market that they may not be able to afford."[1] I do not include competition in this chapter for the following reason.

Competition is a strategy that transcends individuals and organizations. As Boatright clarifies, "no firm would use increased competition as a means for managing conflicts of interest."[2] Rather, it is a choice that corresponds to political actors such as industry regulators and in this regard it constitutes a macrolevel strategy. The problem, as far as we are concerned, is that this takes us into the political arena. Now, I am not suggesting that conflicts of interest have no political implications, but if we open the door to politics here we will probably end up throwing our books at each other. I prefer to keep our discussion to the ethical, i.e., the microlevel and mid-level, as the title of the book promised.

One last observation before we begin. This chapter inevitably serves as a sort of instruction manual or map for managing conflicts of interest. That said, one thing is to study a map and another is to cross the forest. Reality is complex and making good decisions is often difficult, not only because of the temptations we face: discerning the best choice is many times difficult as well. For instance, and as we will soon see, when it comes to the third "E" (escape) one has to judge what is best: to escape a conflict of interest by targeting the duty, the interest that is causing the conflict, or both. Let's say that one decides to target the duty and recuse oneself from the responsibility; this may end up being a mistake, perhaps even a big mistake. How so? Well, maybe the duty is a very consequential one and we are the most qualified, or even the only, person available to perform the duty.

So, let's begin by discussing individual management. And let's do so with the first "E," something everyone concerned with the ethical management of conflicts of interest should do: explore.

EXPLORE (THE FIRST "E" OF INDIVIDUAL MANAGEMENT)

Our first step is to explore whether the organizations we work for and the occupations that sustain us have established rules and policies on conflicts of interest. Typically, we will find this in a code of ethics. Rules and policies in general, and codes of ethics in particular, can positively surprise us regarding the guidance they offer—for instance, they will probably contain concrete instructions on evading conflicts of interest (the second "E," let's recall)—though this is not to say that we should take these rules, policies, and codes as infallible (more on this later).

Take the case of gifts from an organization's clients or suppliers. Gifts from these sources are usually restricted and for a good reason: they can easily create conflicts of interest. After all, when someone gives us something, we feel both grateful and indebted. The following example illustrates this well.

The "gifted" banker. Bob shines at a bank, where he calculates interest rates for mortgages. Christy and Thomas go along to Bob's branch with a dream of their first home. The prospective applicants know well that a single digit can make a big difference to a thirty-year loan. They also know, from the pictures in Bob's office, that he loves to grill. They decide to surprise him mid-application with the hottest new device among barbecue aficionados. Bob wonders if he should accept it.

Bob could spend all the time in the world pondering whether the gift is big enough to influence him, convincing himself that it would make no difference to his professional objectivity, and so on. His life would be much easier, though, if he just opened his employer's code of ethics. If he worked for Bank of America, for instance, Bob would save himself a lot of time, since the bank forbids gifts altogether. In the exact words of its code of ethics: "Associates must not give or receive gifts of money to or from current or prospective customers or suppliers, unless given as part of an approved Bank of America customer satisfaction program."[33] Clearly, Christy and Thomas's gift is not part of an approved Bank of America customer satisfaction program, so Bob would simply have to reject the gift. End of story. He would lose out on the grill, but he would gain peace of mind. (Note in addition the way in which a good code of ethics can be useful and not merely a lifeless bundle of paper.)

Not all organizations regulate conflicts of interest equally, though. If Bob worked instead for, say, Chase, he might be allowed to accept the gift—as long as he answered the following questions in the negative: Did he solicit the gift? Has he received frequent gifts or offers from the same source? Would acceptance of it violate any policies of his business unit or location? Is the gift being given in appreciation for good service as thanks for the company's business? Is this customer, supplier, or company trying to influence or reward him in connection with a business decision or transaction? Is the gift on the list of "non-appropriate" gifts (for instance, does its retail value exceeds US$100)?[4]

If we apply Chase's acceptance criteria to the "gifted" banker, it may be the case that Bob could accept the gift. After all, questions four and five are impossible to answer with absolute certainty. Or can we read people's minds and hearts?

The variety of regulations in circulation invites a further reflection that complicates things further: it is possible that the code of ethics you are subject to is regulating the issue wrongly. We might, for instance, judge—rightly—that Bank of America's flat prohibition of gifts is better than Chase's restrictions, arguing that the latter leaves the door open for conflicts of interest. Consider the amount: a US$100 gift will be high enough for many (if you give me that amount in books, I will be delighted). Hence, it is not enough in itself to follow a code of ethics or some equivalent: the document could be flawed and end up inducing, instead of preventing, conflicts of interest. So, we still have to judge for ourselves whether the regulations are completely sound. But knowing your code of ethics is better than ignoring it. So, explore.

TEXT BOX 6.1: THE THREE LEVELS OF ETHICAL ANALYSIS (AND MANAGEMENT)

In their book chapter "Conflicts of Interest," Norman and MacDonald say that conflicts of interest can be analyzed at three levels, each with its own set of questions:

Microlevel. Which duties does a professional or expert owe to various parties, clients, employers, or the public? What rights does she have to pursue her own interests in the context of selling a service to a client? What should she do when she recognises she is in, or could be perceived to be in, a conflict of interest situation?

Mid-level. How should a firm or some other kind of organisation employing professionals and experts be structured so that the firm itself avoids or manages its conflicts of interest, as well as the conflicts its employees may find themselves in? What rules should it have about conflicts of interest among its employees? How should it teach, monitor, and enforce these rules? Also, what rules, training, and sanctions should professions themselves have concerning the conflicts of interest of their members?

Macrolevel: Why should there be professions and when should putative professional bodies be granted a monopoly on rights to silence (and to punish or expel) practitioners? Contrariwise, when should domains of experts simply be left to ply their trade in the marketplace? Why are government regulations concerning

conflicts of interest appropriate for the private sector? What conflict-of-interest rules and laws are appropriate for public servants,
elected officials, judges, and so on?[5]

The authors further claim that research has moved from the microlevel
to the midlevel, and that it is a good thing. They also call for new
research at the macrolevel (something I am not opposed to, but which,
as I explained, I would rather not touch upon in this book).

EVADE (THE SECOND "E" OF INDIVIDUAL MANAGEMENT)

We have already said a little about the second "E": evade. If you manage
to do this, you will save yourself, well, a conflict of interest—with all that
it entails.

The problem is that not all conflicts of interests can be evaded. Conflicts
of interest are very fertile and can reproduce in spite of the most effective
"contraceptives," against our will and despite our best efforts—except, of
course, for "chastity," which would mean leaving the business and professional world altogether. But most people cannot just leave this world.

The scrupulous auditor. Karl is an accountant at a consulting firm. His
main job is to perform audits and he is very serious about it. Karl is so
scrupulous that when he became an authority in auditing, he put all his
assets in a blind trust. That way he could keep conflicts of interest at bay,
securing the quality of his future work. Karl was leading an audit for a food
corporation when his mobile phone alerted him of a match on a dating app.
It was his future girlfriend (he did not know this yet), who works for the
same food corporation (he did not know this yet either).

As the example illustrates—and as Davis puts it nicely—we cannot
put all our interests, especially the intangible ones, into a blind trust.[6] We
simply cannot. This is why evasion is only one among other options for
managing conflicts of interest.

The fact that some conflicts of interest cannot be evaded is something
to bear in mind when regulating them. Turning to Davis again, "virtually
all professional codes, and many corporate codes of ethics as well, provide
some guidance on how to deal with conflicts of interest. But many [ill-
advisedly] say no more than 'avoid all conflicts of interest.'"[7] Why is this
ill-advised?

If some conflicts of interest cannot be evaded, as the case of the scrupulous auditor shows, then flat prohibitions are both unrealistic and unfair.

They are as unrealistic as flat prohibitions on getting sick would be. Sooner or later people will get sick just like sooner or later people will face a conflict of interest. Flat prohibitions are also unfair to the extent that when the unavoidable conflict of interest appears, the person facing it will nonetheless appear to have acted wrongly.

As those who have studied law will know, one of its fundamental principles is *lex non cogit ad impossibilia*, "the law does not compel a man to do that which is impossible." Any law that violates this principle is invalid. A law, for instance, that commands criminals to time-travel to the past to undo their crimes is not a law at all—even if has gone through all the formalities of one. Well, the same goes for flat prohibitions of conflicts of interest: they are laws that compel a man to do that which is impossible.

Of course, we can and should still say, in codes and other types of regulations, that people should try their very best to evade them. In fact, that is what flat prohibitions aim at. But even then such prohibitions should only be the starting point for stronger policies and measures. Again, evading is just one of the ways to manage conflicts of interest.

Let's, though, say something else about this command to evade conflicts of interest. The scrupulous auditor showed us one way of doing it (putting one's assets in a trust fund), but, depending on the circumstances, there will be other ways too. For instance, the self-employed can evade by asking themselves, before scrutinizing or accepting a new client, if the involvement will create a conflict of interest with another client. And not only the self-employed—those who speak in the name of an organization should ask themselves the same question. Whatever route you have to take to evade a conflict, evade it.

ESCAPE (THE THIRD "E" OF INDIVIDUAL MANAGEMENT)

Let's say that we are already (whether through fault of our own or not) in a conflict of interest. It's time to escape, but how?

The first half of our definition of conflicts of interest gives us the clue: "A situation in which an interest tempts one to disregard an office-, position-, work- or job-related duty." Hence, to escape a conflict of interest, a first option would be to unbind oneself from the duty. In other words, one can try to recuse or disqualify oneself and transfer the duty to someone else ("partial limitation of the fiduciary relationship," as Luebke puts it[8]). If the duty is gone, the situation will be gone as well, since the former is essential to conflicts of interest.

With regard to this, Carson makes the good point that sometimes the sensible thing to do, when recusing oneself, is to not expose (the fourth "E") the conflict of interest.[9] That is, through exposure or disclosure, the conflict of interest can be transferred to the new person in charge, like in the following case.

The eager-to-please assistant. Bertha is the human resources manager of a grocery store chain. She is reviewing applications for an open position in a distant city when she sees a familiar name: her niece Jill. Bertha takes her job very seriously, so immediately delegates this particular task to one of her assistants, Peter, after explaining the situation. Peter, though, likes his boss and knows she will be happy if her niece is hired. He thus feels inclined to hire her regardless of her credentials.

Had Bertha not explained the problem, the eager-to-please assistant would have evaluated the applications objectively—but he cannot anymore. Note that even if Jill is ultimately hired on objective considerations, Bertha will not be out of the woods in terms of conflicts of interest; as the chain's human resources manager, she will inevitably have to make decisions that affect Jill at some point.

This example invites us to consider the other way to escape a conflict of interest: to target the interest, not the duty—more precisely, to keep the latter and get rid of the former. If we make this happen, the conflict of interest will also be gone, since there will be nothing remaining to tempt us to disregard the duty. In the case of the eager-to-please assistant, this would entail asking Jill to withdraw her application or refusing to consider it altogether.

Divesting oneself of intangible interests, by the way, is usually harder than divesting oneself of tangible ones. Assets can be sold or, as we already mentioned, put in a blind trust. In the case of intangible interests, though, this may be impossible or simply absurd. It is impossible, for instance, to cut all ties with our family—after all, we share the same blood. One can cut all contact, but not all ties. It would be absurd, on the other hand, to expect someone to end a friendship or terminate a marriage. When this is the case, attention should be placed again on the duty, not on the interest.

Let's say that one can neither divest oneself of the interest nor recuse oneself from the duty. In our example, imagine that Jill refused to withdraw her application, that disregarding her application would be unwise because of her outstanding qualifications, and that Bertha has no one to whom to delegate the decision. Now, imagine that Jill's hiring is fundamental for the survival of the company. In extreme cases like this, the wisest, albeit far from the easiest, decision would be to resign from our office or job. Yes, the ethics of conflicts of interest can demand that much from us.

Resigning, of course, will not always be necessary. It might even be an overreaction, an excess of scrupulousness. If resignation is overzealous, and escape becomes otherwise impossible, one can turn to another option: to summon the fourth "E" of individual management, i.e., to expose the conflict of interest.

TEXT BOX 6.2: DAVIS ON "THE BEST APPROACH"

After giving his own recipe for the individual management of conflicts of interest, Davis presents what he calls the "the best approach":

> What should be done about a conflict of interest depends on all the circumstances, including the relative importance of the decision in question; the alternatives available; the wishes of the principal, client, employer, or the like; the law; and any relevant code of ethics, professional or institutional. Some conflicts of interest should be escaped, others should be disclosed, and a few should be managed.[10]

Davis, as usual, is on to something. However, I think it is worth offering a few qualifications. First, not all conflicts of interest will be solved in the same way, using the same "E" of individual management. Second, the approach will depend on the circumstances (which, for instance, can condition the inescapability of the conflict of interest). Third, the more information we have, the better.

The "best approach," then, is not an additional "E"—unless we were to add an "I" to the five "E"s of individual management: when facing a conflict of interest, *inform* yourself as much as possible. Conflicts of interest do not occur in a vacuum and without information proper management will prove impossible. That said, I think that this potential "I" is implicit—perhaps even explicit in the case of regulations—in our five "E"s.

The first "E" (explore) asks that we inform ourselves regarding how conflicts of interest are regulated in our occupation or organization. But applying the other "E"s will also require information. I would need it, for instance, when deciding if I can escape a conflict of interest. How could I judge the situation otherwise? Thus, we should not be led astray by Davis's "best approach." There are no more than five "E"s, but they all demand information.

EXPOSE (THE FOURTH "E" OF INDIVIDUAL MANAGEMENT)

Let's now saw that we did not (whether through fault of our own or not) escape a conflict of interest. What next? At the very least, we should come clean and expose the situation to the principal. This—which Luebke regard as "the more common course of action"[11] when dealing with conflicts of interest—gives the person in question the chance to make a decision. More specifically, this gives the person the chance to dissolve the conflict (by assigning the duty to another employee, looking for another supplier, etcetera) or to consent to the situation despite the risks. Note that in the latter case the conflict of interest will not disappear, with all that this entails.

The exposing or disclosing should be done properly to be considered valid, though, as Davis points out.[12] For instance, we do not want to communicate the conflict of interest we are facing in such a way that the other party not only fails to recognize the seriousness of the situation but also misunderstands the whole scenario and thinks that there is a concurrence instead of a conflict of interests.

The opportunist purchasing officer. Mike is a purchasing officer at a grocery store. His inner entrepreneur has long dreamed of running a microbrewery. Finally, his opportunity arrives: a local microbrewery is on sale, so he buys it—but decides to stay on at his job for now. At the grocery store, the time has come to select the brands that will fill the beer section next season. After adding his own brand on the list, he informs his boss of the conflict of interest with the words: "This brewery is so good that I have invested my own money in it."

This is as lame a disclosure as it gets. To expose a conflict of interest properly, one should instead be as clear as possible, ensuring that the other party fully recognizes what is going on and how his or her own interest is at stake. Not only that, but one should communicate the other party's basic options.

We saw earlier that while it is the ethical thing to do, exposing a conflict of interest does not eliminate it. Not only that, but, as Norman and MacDonald point out (based on works by Daylian M. Cain et al.[13] and others), empirical research has found that doing so increases the probabilities of doing a bad job (of dishonoring our duty). These findings, Norman and MacDonald argue, suggests two things:

(1) that clients are unlikely to be able to effectively use professional disclosures of conflicts of interest to correctly discount advise they

are given, and (2) that professionals making such disclosures may, in fact, give more biased advice than professionals who fail to make such disclosures.[14]

The second point, I think, may be due to rationalization—the human power to "justify" the unjust, i.e., to convince ourselves of the morality of something that, deep down, we know is immoral. The temptation to yield to the interest remains and we tell ourselves that we already did what ethics required—namely, to expose the situation and to obtain informed consent, and that anything beyond that will be an excess of scrupulousness. It may also be the result of an overconfidence in our abilities to manage temptations. We think we can do our job properly, confident in our ethics and experience. The fact is that, as the abovementioned research shows, we are more vulnerable to moral failure than we think.

This empirical research, though, should by no means lead to the condemnation or discouragement of exposing a conflict of interest. Transparency is fundamental not only for business ethics but for ethics in general. It is, at a minimum, a way of respecting others, of treating them as ends and not merely as means, as Kant would put it.[15] Instead, the research should lead to less informed consent and to more requests for removal, resignation, and so on. It should also lead to more care on the part of the person facing the conflict of interest, to more organizational measures, etcetera.

EXECUTE (THE FIFTH "E" OF INDIVIDUAL MANAGEMENT)

So, we did not evade the conflict of interest, did not escape it either, and, after actualizing the fourth "E" (expose), obtained informed consent. What now? We must summon the fifth "E" of individual management: execute. Execute what? Not the other party (that would be immoral, I hope you agree), but the office- or job-related duty.

Remember that exposing the conflict of interest does not make it disappear. The duty and the conflicting interest remain, and they struggle to resolve the conflict in their favor. Well, like in any typical moral problem where a duty fights an interest, one must choose the former.

If we tried to evade and escape the conflict of interest, we will already have chosen the duty over the interest. By trying to evade and escape the situation, we recognize the primacy of the former—otherwise, we would not have even tried and would simply have served our interest immediately. Now it is time to execute the duty.

This is the final test, and it will come at a price. We may lose an opportunity to favor ourselves or a loved one, but what is at stake on the other end of the scale is more important: someone's dignity and general happiness, among other things (as discussed in the last chapter).

Boatright says something similar when talking about the commitment to be objective—a commitment that requires "a strong character that resists the temptation to earn more."[16] It requires a strong character because it is not easy to let an opportunity go. Well, the ethics of conflicts of interest demands that we let opportunities go. We must remind ourselves that even if the interest is legitimate, the opportunity is not.

Once we have prioritized the work-related duty, our challenge is to focus on it and do our best. We ought to push and doubt ourselves more than usual. One way of doing this is devoting more time to the particular issue. We should ask ourselves what we would we if we had no interest at stake.

Something we may want to clarify is how mechanical the task is. If it requires judgment, it would be advisable to ask a colleague to look at the issue. In other words, it is wise to look for independent judgment. We may have decided to prioritize the duty, but our judgment can still be affected by the interest—it can convince us that the best course of action is actually the second-best or even the worst. This is less possible (or altogether impossible) when the task is mechanical, since the requirement will be far clearer.

The tangled business development executive. Micah is a talented business development executive for a local coffee shop. After rigorous market research, he has concluded that the company should open a second shop in a trendy area. This requires renting a space. The problem? He owns what can be regarded as the best spot available. He sends the proposal to the CEO and does not forget to expose the conflict of interest. The CEO, trusting him, approves the project, but he still hesitates about whether his judgment has been clouded.

Since Micah cannot know, with complete certainty, if his business proposal is the best one for the company, his judgment may be compromised. It is in precisely this type of case that independent judgment is needed. This judgment may come from one's own team or from outside. It is it from outside, then it might not come for free (if we do not have a friend who is an expert in the field and who is open to looking at the case without charging for it, then somebody will have to pay the bill). But we have already established that the ethical management of conflicts of interest comes at a price—but in the short term, ethics often does.

These are the five "E"s of individual management: explore, evade, escape, expose, and execute. Now it is time to discuss the ABC of organizational management: align, build walls, and codify.

TEXT BOX 6.3: NOT PUTTING OTHERS IN A CONFLICT OF INTEREST

Before starting the discussion of organizational management, let's say something about putting others in a conflict of interest. Here is an example I heard first hand.

Where I live, if you do not take your statutory annual leave, your employer must pay you your regular monthly salary plus two additional ones (don't ask why). A friend of mine had not taken her leave for years and saw the opportunity to gain some extra money. The law, though, was not clear about whether she could claim that money at any time or only at the end of the labor relationship, whenever that may be. She said: "I sent the request to the human resources manager. She is my friend, so I think it will work out." I imagine that, deep down, she knew there was something problematic about her request: she put her friend in a conflict of interest. Could she had done otherwise? Most probably, yes. The fact is that instead of pondering the situation, she was content for her friend to resolve it.

Now, what is the problem with this? The problem is simple: putting someone in a conflict of interest is putting that person in a moral problem.

Another example. Some months ago I was in the middle of a mortgage application. I had been negotiating with the developer and with the bank, when Covid-19 broke out. My doubt was: should I go ahead with the whole thing or quit, considering the risk that the project would fall through? I needed to talk to someone who could tell me how financially strong the developer was. Then I remembered I had a friend who held a senior position at the bank. After explaining the situation, I told her: "I should have sent my application to your branch." She answered: "I prefer not to involve family or friends in my area. That would create conflicts of interest." Believe it or not, I, the future author of a book on conflicts of interest, did not notice I was putting my friend in one.

To express the problem in another way, putting someone in a conflict of interest equates to promoting immoral actions, and promoting immorality is, logically, immoral.

ALIGN (THE "A" OF ORGANIZATIONAL MANAGEMENT)

First, a clarification. We examined the possibility of organizations them-selves (as opposed to their members) facing conflicts of interest in a previous chapter. To speak of organizational management does not undermine that. The point is to present measures that can only be implemented at the organizational level to fight individual conflicts of interest.

As Boatright puts it, alignment involves countering conflicts of interest "by incentives that align the person's interest with the interests of those to be served."[17] But how? Through the creation of a new interest that is strong enough to overpower the interest that tempts us to disregard the position- or job-related duty. If created properly, the new interest will change the situation in such a way that it becomes in our interest to serve our employer or client's interest. Naturally, this strategy also promises to secure the duty—a "win-win situation," so to speak.

The single example Boatright provides is, regrettably, a controversial one: high executive compensation linked to performance (stock grants, options, and so on). The idea is that the executive, who explicitly or implicitly has promised shareholders to lead the company to success, will be unshakably motivated to do her duty to her best ability. If another personal interest emerges that tempts her to dishonor this promise, the interest in the company's success will most probably be stronger. As a consequence, the chances of a mismanaged conflict of interest will decrease or even disappear.

The example is controversial for at least two reasons. The first is the moral status of high executive compensation itself. This is a very hot topic in business ethics, especially at a time when this compensation is at a historic high and when the CEO-to-typical-worker compensation ratio is also as lop-sided as it has ever been. According to the Economic Policy Institute, the average income of a top CEO is around $17 million, having grown by 1,007.5 percent since 1978. Now compare this growth to that of the average worker's wage: 11.9 percent. Consider also the CEO-to-typical worker compensation ratio, which was 20-to-1 in 1965 and is now 278-to-1.[18]

Of course, one may argue that there is nothing unjust in this, but I doubt that the argument would be valid or sound. Now, it is not my intention to discuss the ethics of CEOs' compensation. Rather, my point is twofold. First, that top executives are already being paid very well, but are not managing conflicts of interest any better (or is there any evidence that they are?). Second, if we assume that the compensation is unjust, Boatright is simply solving one moral problem by reinforcing another one. I assume that Boatright sees no moral problem in high compensation (otherwise he would not have proposed this in the first place), but his implication that it is unproblematic should not go uncontested.

The second reason why the example is controversial is its elitist nature. As Carson has argued, conflicts of interest as a topic in business ethics—unlike corporate social responsibility—has the merit of appealing to people at all levels.[19] Every worker will face a conflict of interest eventually. Issues to do with corporate social responsibility, on the contrary, are often the preserve of top executives. By using this single example, Boatright is, intentionally or unintentionally, adding to the elitist trend in business ethics (because truly high compensation only makes sense at the highest levels of management).

If we want to add alignment as an organizational strategy to prevent conflicts of interest, we must think of different proposals. But what kind of interest can we establish that could overpower other tangible and intangible interests? I can think of two. First, a moral interest through education. If the members of an organization care about living an ethical life, a good training program on conflicts of interest should reinforce the idea that it is in their moral interest to manage them well. Second, a prudential interest through regulations. Before discussing regulations, though, let's discuss walls.

BUILD WALLS (THE "B" OF ORGANIZATIONAL MANAGEMENT)

By building walls I do not mean reversing the trend in home—and office, for that matter—renovations of promoting "open spaces." In other words, I am not referring to physical walls (although it may entail this as well) but to institutional walls. That is, the blocking of the flow of information between units or teams when that flow can lead to conflicts of interest. This is especially important in companies and industries that offer different services to different customers. The financial industry in particular has a need for this—which is why, in the United States and other countries, the division of services was for decades regulated by law.

The story began with the financial crisis of 1929. As part of the regulations that followed the crisis, in 1933 the U.S. Congress forbade commercial banks from selling stocks or insurance. As a result, Americans did not see any banks selling insurance until 1999, when the *Glass-Steagall Act* repealed the prohibition. The consequences? We suffered them in 2008, when history repeated itself through a new financial crisis. In fact, one could say that the Global Recession was, in great measure, the result of a multiplication of conflicts of interest that the regulatory repeal ignited—and the systematic mismanagement compounded.

Fortunately, we do not necessarily need a law to compartmentalize the services of organizations. Organizations in most sectors can do this themselves by building the so-called "Chinese walls." As *A Dictionary of Finance and Banking* it defines it, a Chinese wall is:

> A notional information barrier between the parts of a business, notably between the market-making part of a stockbroking firm and the broking part. It would clearly not be in investors' interests for brokers to persuade their clients to buy investments from them for no other reason than that the market makers in the firm, expecting a fall in price, were anxious to sell them.[20]

The accounting world is also famous for its need for this kind of wall. Accounting firms usually provide auditing and consulting services for the same clients. The problem is that the consulting service is much more profitable and assigned at the client's behest. When the time for auditing arrives, accounting firms may feel tempted to be lenient with the firms in order to keep the client and their consulting custom. This explains the call for breaking up the two sides of the business within each company which, as Boatright says, will strengthen "the independence and integrity of each unit"[21]—and will reduce conflicts of interest as a result.

An organization does not need to offer different services to have the need for this kind of walls. Two competing clients are enough. Imagine, for instance, a marketing company with two competing clients. A way of managing this would through the creation of two teams of marketers who commit themselves to not talking to each other about their marketing plans. Of course, this in itself is not enough: the teams should be equally competent. Putting the best marketers in one team (due, say, to the bigger size of one client) will automatically signify a mismanaged conflict of interest.

The term "Chinese wall," by the way, opens the door to another ethical discussion. Is the term offensive? The most famous argument against its use was made in the 1980s by a Chinese-American judge: Harry W. Low. Justice Low did something else as well—he proposed using another term, "ethics wall."

Considering that the term "Chinese wall" is now widely considered to be offensive, and that "ethics wall" is not only offensive to no one but much more direct and clear as well, I see no reason not to abandon the former in favor of the latter (and, while we're about it, *Oxford English*

Dictionary can change the corresponding entry. At the very least, it should acknowledge the alternative term after explaining the problematic nature of "Chinese wall").

TEXT BOX 6.4: JUSTICE HARRY W. LOW'S CRITIQUE OF TERM "CHINESE WALL"

"I write to express my profound objection to the use of this phrase.

The term has an ethnic focus which many would consider a subtle form of linguistic discrimination. Certainly, the continued use of the term would be insensitive to the ethnic identity of the many persons of Chinese descent. Modern courts should not perpetuate the biases which creep into language from outmoded, and more primitive, ways of thought.

Aside from this discriminatory flavor, the term 'Chinese Wall' is being used to describe a barrier of silence and secrecy. The barrier itself may work to further the cause of ethics in litigation; but the term ascribed to that barrier will necessarily be associated with constraints on the freedom of open communication. To employ in this context the image of the Great Wall of China, one of the magnificent wonders of the world and a structure of great beauty, is particularly inappropriate. One can imagine the response to the negative use of the images of the Eiffel Tower, the Great Pyramid of Cheops, or the Colossus of Rhodes.

Finally, 'Chinese Wall' is not even an architecturally accurate metaphor for the barrier to communication. . . . Such a barrier functions as a hermetic seal to prevent two-way communication between two groups. The Great Wall of China, on the other hand, was only a one-way barrier. It was built to keep outsiders out—not to keep insiders in.

It is necessary to raise a clenched cry for jettisoning the outmoded legal jargon of a bygone time. If the image of a wall must be used, perhaps 'ethics wall' is more suitable phraseology."[22]

CODIFY (THE "C" OF ORGANIZATIONAL MANAGEMENT)

Another organizational action to fight conflicts of interest is to regulate or codify them. The most common way of doing this is through a code of ethics.

Business and professional codes of ethics are a somewhat new phenomenon. They emerged in the twentieth century, gaining momentum in the 1970s and 1980s. Rather than any single reason, there were a variety of factors behind this: honest concern for ethics, shock and fear after big corporate scandals, new laws and regulations, corporate image, bandwagon-jumping, and so on. Whatever the reason for their reproduction, codes of ethics are now everywhere and are seemingly here to stay.

The reasons why codes of ethics emerged do not necessarily coincide with their justification. Why are codes of ethics necessary or convenient? How are they helpful? How do they serve ethics? The justification of business (and other kinds of) codes of ethics is a difficult business. For instance, the debate around their effectiveness (not a philosophical question but an empirical one) is still open.[23] Still, one may give the following basic justification for having a code of ethics—even under the assumption that they are not as effective as one would wish.

The justification is the following: a good code of ethics offers moral guidance to its users. At a minimum, it informs them about the typical moral problems one encounters at work and the way to deal with them properly. What problems in particular? Well, the same topics that appear again and again in the same codes of ethics.

George C. S. Benson, for instance, in his study of codes of ethics, lists the following topics as somewhat recurrent (some more than others): corporate relations with employees, inter-employee relations on ethics, whistle-blowing, effects of corporations on the environment, commercial bribery, insider information, antitrust issues, accounting issues, consumer relations, political activities and contributions, and, yes, conflicts of interest.[24]

Of these topics, conflicts of interest is, to no one's surprise, one of the most common in codes of ethics. In his article, Benson compiles some examples, starting with the way Great Western Financial Corporation defines conflicts of interest:

> A conflict of interest exists where an employee has a personal financial interest or other relationship outside Great Western that is or could be adverse to the best interests of Great Western, even though such interest or relationship does not result in any financial loss to Great Western. A conflict may exist irrespective of the intent of the employee.[25]

Thanks to codes of ethics, their users (for instance, a new worker) learn something about conflicts of interest. Specifically, they learn what a conflict of interest is and that it is something they must take seriously.

Yet, users of codes of ethics not only learn what conflicts of interest are but also ways to manage them. To follow another of Benson's example, in its code of ethics Citicorp forbids workers from dealing with any vendor or customer for personal gain, which would constitute a mismanaged conflict of interest.

It is not my intention to outline what Benson says regarding conflicts of interest, but these very brief references to his work invite another reflection: the regulation of conflicts of interest in codes of ethics tends to be flawed. For instance, the definition that Benson picks up on but does not comment upon (Great Western) is less than ideal. In short, Great Western identifies conflicts of interest with conflicting interest. With this, though, I am getting ahead of what we will discuss in detail in the next chapter: the most common mistakes in the way conflicts of interest are regulated in codes of ethics.

CHAPTER SUMMARY

In this chapter, I outlined and discussed how to manage conflicts of interest. I covered the five "E"s of individual management and the ABC of organizational management.

At the individual level, the chapter first suggested exploring how conflicts of interest are regulated in each of our jobs and occupations. Is there a code of ethics that governs your job? If so, it will help to know what this code says—without taking its content dogmatically. As an example, the chapter presented the case of the "gifted" banker.

Next, I discussed the necessity to evade, whenever possible, conflicts of interest. We can be negligent with regard to them, and this is a bad thing. It is bad because conflicts of interest, as we have said many times, invite us to act immorally. Most space, though, was devoted to unavoidable conflicts of interest. This is to erase flat prohibitions from regulations. The scrupulous auditor made this point clear.

After evading, I spoke of the need to escape, again whenever possible, conflicts of interest. We saw that there are two ways in which we can do this. First, by untying ourselves from the work-related duty—for instance, by assigning the duty to a colleague. That this should not always be done through exposure was made clear with the assistant under pressure. Second, by divesting oneself from the interest. The chapter also mentioned an extreme but sometimes necessary way to escape a conflict of interest: resigning.

Next in line was exposing the conflict. Exposure gives the other party the chance to make a decision. This, though, should be done properly, as the opportunist purchasing officer illustrated. I offered some specific conditions to achieve this. I also clarified that exposure does not eliminate the conflict and that it may even increase the probabilities of mismanaging it. Despite this, exposure is the ethical thing to do.

The fifth and final "E" of individual management involved executing the office or position-related duty as professionally as possible—even at the price of your interest. This also means making an extra effort in the case at hand, so as to secure the quality of what one has committed oneself to do. I also discussed an additional measure if the duty at hand required judgment: asking for a second opinion. The tangled business development executive supported this.

At the organizational level, the chapter discussed the ABC of management: align, build walls, and codify. Regarding the first, it discussed Boatright's suggestion of high executive compensation and why it is a problematic way to align. In preference, I suggested a purer alignment: education plus regulations.

Before regulations, though, I discussed the compartmentalization of units or teams: building walls. I did so with a special focus on "ethics walls," which I suggest should be used in preference to the offensive "Chinese walls." The challenge is to ensure that the information inside a company remains where it should be, which is another way of preventing conflicts of interest.

Finally, I moved on to codifying, the "C" in the ABC, with an emphasis on the convenience of codes of ethics. I talked a little bit about their history, justification, and their most common content—which usually includes conflicts of interests. I briefly considered, as well, some real examples and started noticing how their regulation can be defective (as I will evaluate in detail in the next chapter).

In the middle of all this, I explored the three levels of ethical analysis of conflicts of interest, Davis' "best approach" to managing them, the importance of not putting others in conflicts of interest, and Judge Low's critique of the term "Chinese wall."

I hope this chapter satisfied the doers among you. If you are one of them, you may also find the next chapter interesting: it contains guidance on how to regulate conflicts of interest properly.

QUESTIONS AND EXERCISES FOR REFLECTION

1. If you work (or have worked) for an organization, does it has a code of ethics or some equivalent document? Does this document regulate conflicts of interest?

2. Is it always possible to evade conflicts of interest?
3. How can one escape a conflict of interest?
4. Is it always advisable to expose a conflict of interest?
5. What does the fifth "E" of individual management refer to? What is one supposed to execute?
6. What do you think of Boatright's suggestion of aligning interests through high executive compensation?
7. If you work (or have worked) for an organization, is there some sort of "ethics wall" in place there? Should there be one? Explain.
8. Can you think of a new "E," or any other letter, of individual management? And another way to manage conflicts of interest at the organizational level?
9. Is there any suggestion you would like to make about this chapter? How would you improve the proposals for managing conflicts of interest it contains?
10. Think of the last conflict of interest you faced. How did you manage it? What have you done differently since? Tell your story, even if it is one of failure.

Chapter 7

CONFLICTS OF INTEREST
IN CODES OF ETHICS

A s we saw in the previous chapter, the typical code of ethics includes a section on conflicts of interest. The way they regulate them, though, is rarely pristine. Consider, for instance, how Alphabet regulates conflicts of interest in its code of ethics:[1]

> When you are in a business situation in which competing loyalties could cause you to pursue a personal benefit for you, your friends, or your family at the expense of Alphabet or our users, you may be faced with a conflict of interest. All of us should avoid conflicts of interest and circumstances that reasonably present the appearance of a conflict.
>
> When considering a course of action, ask yourself whether the action you're considering could create an incentive for you, or appear to others to create an incentive for you, to benefit yourself, your friends or family, or an associated business at the expense of Alphabet. If the answer is "yes," the action you're considering is likely to create a conflict of interest situation, and you should avoid it.[2]

What do you think about this? Does this regulate conflicts of interest well?

To answer this, we need, first of all, to return to the questions we have been addressing in throughout this book—the questions regarding the definition, classification, moral status, and proper management of conflicts of interest. Then we need to look for the corresponding answers in the code of ethics we are reading. To be more specific, we need to compare our answers with the way a code defines, classifies, assesses, and establishes how to manage conflicts of interest.

In the case of Alphabet, the company defines conflicts of interest as conflicting interests, does not explain why they are morally problematic, and restricts their management to one rule: evade them. So, given all you now know about conflicts of interest, what do you think about this treatment? I imagine you will agree that it is not the sharpest.

Alphabet is not alone. When we review the way codes of ethics regulate conflicts of interest, we find these and other problems. The aim of this chapter is to highlight these common errors—focusing on *business* codes of ethics. This is not with the intention of mere "error signaling" (the theoretical equivalent to "virtue signalling"), but with the constructive intention of improving these same regulations—and of inspiring future ones.

In the first two sections of this chapter, I focus on the way codes of ethics define conflicts of interest, highlighting several ways in which codes err (omissions, flawed definitions, etcetera). In the third section, I deal with the classification of conflicts of interest classification and look at how codes of ethics tend to focus on extrinsic conflicts of interest—bypassing the intrinsic type. In the fourth, I discuss the error of not explaining why conflicts of interest are morally problematic. In the fifth section, I look at how codes of ethics establish the proper management of conflicts of interest. The mistake here, as we will see, lies in highlighting one or two management measures, like evade and expose, while ignoring the other available ways of managing conflicts of interest. In the sixth section, I examine the tendency among codes of ethics to regulate conflicts of interest outside the sections devoted to conflicts of interest themselves. This leads us on to the seventh section, where I explore a similar problem: the regulation of conflicts of interest outside codes of ethics, i.e., in independent policies and similar documents. Finally, in the eighth section, I gather together the lessons learned from this critical study of codes of ethics so that readers with the power to rectify, draft, or commission a code of ethics do not repeat them.

Readers will leave this chapter prepared to assess how codes of ethics in their organizations (or professions, occupations, etc.) regulate conflicts of interest—and ready to propose or oversee improvements.

FLAWED DEFINITIONS 1: CONFLICTING INTERESTS

When it comes to defining conflicts of interest, codes of ethics can err in more than one way: through omissions, flawed definitions, or even multiple definitions.

By omissions, I mean the error of not providing a singled-out definition. These omissions, though, are never absolute. A definition is virtually
always there even if it is not overt, intermingled with the rules for the
proper management of conflicts of interest. Take this example from JP
Morgan Chase:

> You are responsible for avoiding activities or relationships that might
> affect your objectivity in making decisions as a JP Morgan Chase
> employee and raising potential conflicts through controls, disclosures,
> or other appropriate steps. Never permit your personal interest to con-
> flict—or appear to conflict—with our Company's interests.[3]

This code of ethics does not include a straightforward definition of conflicts of interest. There is a definition, but it is mixed with (and thus must
be extracted from) the instructions for their management: "A conflict of
interest is a situation in which your personal interest conflicts with the
company's interests."

Leaving aside the accuracy of the definition (more on that next), the
omission of a singled-out definition is problematic for the following reason:
users of the code can come away without a clear idea of what it is that they
are supposed to avoid or, more broadly speaking, to manage judiciously.
The user will probably wonder: "What exactly are these conflicts of interests I am supposed to avoid?"

When codes of ethics include a singled-out, explicit definition, it is
often flawed. The most common error is the conflation of conflicts of interest with conflicting interests. Examples can be found in the implicit definition of JP Morgan Chase, and the explicit ones of companies such as Nestlé:
"A Conflict of Interest occurs when personal interests of an employee or
the interests of a third party compete with the interests of Nestlé."[4]

As we saw earlier in this book, all conflicts of interest contain conflicting interests, but not all conflicting interests are conflicts of interest.
For instance, employees have an interest in earning more; and employers,
an interest in reducing the company's expenses, but we would be wrong
to call the latter a conflict of interest. A conflict of interest, let's recall, is
a situation in which an interest tempts one to disregard an office-, posi-
tion-, job-, or work-related duty—a situation that threatens the interest
of someone else. The existence of such a duty is fundamental. By defining conflicts of interest as conflicting interests, companies are not merely
making a theoretical mistake, but are asking their members to avoid situations that are not morally problematic—and may unfairly sanction them
if they do not.

Other times, codes include multiple definitions—such as that of the Alibaba Group:

> [1] A conflict of interest occurs when Employees' private interests interfere in any way, or only appear to interfere, with the interests of Alibaba Group. [2] A conflict arises when Employees take actions or have interests that make it difficult for employees to perform their work or duties assigned by Alibaba Group in an objective, unbiased and effective manner. [3] A conflict of interest may arise from an Employee's business or personal relationship with a costumer, supplier, competitor, business partner, or other employee, if that relationship impairs the Employee's objective business judgment.[5]

Three definitions in one paragraph! First: conflicts of interest as conflicting interests. Second: conflicts of interest as I have defined them in this book. Third: conflicts of interest as Davis defines them (judgment-focused definition). The chances of confusing users of the code, I bet you will agree, are high.

TEXT BOX 7.1: DO CODES OF ETHICS MAKE A DIFFERENCE?

In a comprehensive study on the effectiveness of business codes of ethics, Muel Kaptein and Mark S. Schwartz (2008) show us how the research around the effectiveness of codes of ethics yields confusing and even contradictory results. Twenty-eight publications speak of a significant positive impact of codes of ethics in organizations, thirteen speak instead of a weak impact, twenty-six regard codes of ethics as innocuous, eleven observe mixed results, and one study notes a negative impact. In light of this somewhat harsh data, Kaptien and Schwartz give the following recommendations for boards and management:

> First, business codes, as one layer of the house of codes for business, should be regarded as a part of a broader program for managing conduct and stakeholder relationships. A code is not an instrument that stands in isolation of others and it could even be said that in and of itself it is meaningless: the process of developing and implementing the code is pivotal. Second, the effectiveness of business codes will depend on many mediating and moderating factors that may even within one organization; effectively developing and implementing a business code requires taking these

factors into account in each individual division. Third, a factor should be drawn between the quality of a business code—the judgment about its content—and the effectiveness of a code—the judgment about the impact of its content. Fourth, the content of a business code is the basis for determining the indicators for measuring its effectiveness: the behaviour that is addressed in the code is the behaviour that is expected. Fifth, in order to measure the effectiveness of a business code, management should take into account the factors that are presented in this paper. Finally, measuring the effectiveness of a business code requires multiple methods and sources of data.[6]

FLAWED DEFINITIONS 2: NARROW INTEREST

Consider these three corporate definitions of conflicts of interest:

- Alphabet: "[A conflict of interest is] A business situation in which competing loyalties could cause you to pursue a personal benefit for you, your friends, or your family at the expense of Alphabet or our users."[7]
- Microsoft: "Conflicts of interest can arise when our personal relationships or financial interests overlap with our job responsibilities."[8]
- Pfizer: "A conflict of interest arises when you place your personal, social, financial, or political interests before the interests of the company."[9]

Now, remember how, as we saw earlier in the book, any interest can create a conflict of interest. This being the case, it might be argued that the quoted definitions are afflicted by a fourth kind of error: a narrow definition of conflicts of interest resulting from a narrow definition of interest.

In the case of Alphabet, the company's definition of the interest that can cause a conflict of interest mistakenly excludes interests such as those of love for one's country or resentment toward a person—or even toward an animal. We discussed, in chapter 4, some examples of these types of interests, like the nationalist financial analyst, the broken-hearted photographer, and the resentful dog walker. Of course, if we were to interpret "personal benefit" broadly, we might argue that the nationalist financial analyst benefitted—through the joy of helping a company from his beloved country. Fair enough. Still, this leaves the door open for differing interpretations and, thus, necessitates a line of defense on the part of the person who mis-managed the conflict of interest: "What did I gain by recommending that company? Neither I nor my friends or family have money invested in it," that person will say in his or her defense.

In turn, Microsoft also presents a narrow definition of the interest: as "personal relationships or financial interests." Perhaps, it was the company's intention to say "personal interests," but in choosing "personal relation-ships" they preclude conflicts of interests that are motivated by, say, rela-tionships that are not personal in the ordinary sense of the word.

Carson presents an interesting example that in the eyes of Microsoft would not be considered a conflict of interest: "I am sorely tempted to hire someone simply because he is from the same town as my grandfather or because he has the first name of 'Elvis.'"[10] In this example, the person has no personal relationship with the applicant. Under Microsoft's definition, though, this person would not be in a conflict of interest. More precisely, she will be in a conflict of interest, and may potentially even mismanage it, yet she will be off the hook, so to speak, as a worker of Microsoft.

Finally, in its attempt to include all types of interests that might create a conflict of interest, Pfizer sets out a broad list: "personal, social, financial, or political interests." But what if the interest is, say, not political but reli-gious? Returning to the classic example on hiring, an HR manager, say, may be tempted to hire an underqualified candidate, or not hire the best-qualified one, because of her own religious beliefs.

One might argue that I am making a storm in a teacup, but even if the risk posed by a narrow definition of interest were not that bad in practice, why not strive for perfection when it can be reached? Here, "perfection" is approached through simplicity: instead of listing the types of interests that can create a conflict of interest, codes of ethics might be better advised simply to speak of "any interest." In the case of Microsoft, the amended definition would read like this: "Conflicts of interest can arise when any interest overlaps with our job responsibilities." (Now that we are here, we might as well also suggest that instead of saying "overlaps with," Microsoft would be better to say "makes it difficult to honor.")

BLIND SPOT: INTRINSIC CONFLICTS OF INTEREST

Moving beyond definitions (but not leaving them behind), another mistake that codes of ethics tend to make in the regulation of conflicts of interest is to restrict them to the extrinsic type.

Remember one of our discussions regarding the classification of conflicts of interest. The ones most people recognize are the so-called extrinsic conflicts of interest—i.e., conflicts of interest that emerge from an interest extrinsic to the job, office, work, or position. A typical case in point is that of one friend who applies for a position on which the other friend is meant to decide.

The fact is that many conflicts of interest emerge from interests that are intrinsic to the job, such as the interest to ascend in the organizational structure, to punish a colleague, or to defend a policy in which our pride is invested. This group of conflicts is as common and as problematic as the other group, and thus it also deserves attention.

Almost all codes of ethics disregard intrinsic interests, especially in the examples they offer to help users recognize the supposedly most common conflicts of interest. For instance, Cisco lists the following "common situations that can lead to a Conflict of Interest": "work outside Cisco," "personal relationships," "external boards," "external investments," and other activities such as "development of outside inventions or other intellectual property" and "speaking engagements, publications, endorsements."[11]

By "work outside Cisco," the company refers to the likes of outside work related to the employee's responsibilities at Cisco. By "personal relationships," it refers to situations such as family members who work for a Cisco competitor, partner, customer, and so on. By "external boards," it refers to joining the boards of for- or nonprofit organizations, etcetera. By "external investments," it refers to situations like "investment in a private company that is a Cisco competitor, partner, costumer, supplier, or potential candidate for acquisition."[12] And so forth.

Close inspection of the list will reveal that all items are instances of extrinsic conflicts of interest. At this point, Cisco narrows its focus further, presenting examples of hypothetical situations where conflicts of interest appear—and confirming their apparent blind spot for intrinsic conflicts of interest. More specifically, the company raises and answers the following questions: "What if I want to do some consulting work with another technology company?" "What if a family member also works at Cisco?" "What if you or a family member is an investor or principal in an outside company that does business with Cisco or our customers or other parties?"[13] Again, all of these questions point to extrinsic conflicts of interest. In fact, it is as if the second class did not exist or was not a problem for Cisco, when it certainly does and could well be: intrinsic conflicts of interest are as problematic as extrinsic ones. After all, they are both conflicts of interest.

There are other companies that go further and limit conflicts of interest to the extrinsic type not just through examples, but directly. One such company is Chevron: "Conflicts of interest may occur when an individual's *outside activities or personal interests* [emphasis added] conflict or appear to conflict with his or her responsibilities."[14]

One may wonder: What is the problem? The problem is that the user of the code of ethics may end up unable to identify a whole class of conflicts of interest. Now, if conflicts of interest are not identified, the chances of mismanaging them, with all that mismanagement entails, are very high. Moreover, this paves the way for abuse on the part of those the code addresses: a worker could purposely mismanage an intrinsic conflict of interest while claiming that he did not break the code of ethics.

TEXT BOX 7.2: REGULATING INTRINSIC CONFLICTS OF INTEREST

We just saw that intrinsic conflicts of interest are simply ignored in codes of ethics. Is this just a blind spot, or is there a deeper reason behind it? In "Comparing Conflicts of Interest Across de Professions," Stark says something that suggests the existence of a deeper reason:

> For a long time, scholars of conflict of interest typically have concerned themselves only with the first type, when the encumbering interest arises outside of role. For if the second type—when the impairing interest arises within role—were treated as actionable conflicts of interest, all professionals would be in conflict of interest all the time.[15]

Thus, the underlying reason for the absence of intrinsic conflicts of interest in codes of ethics would be—if I understand Stark correctly—that they are not, as he says, "actionable," i.e., they cannot be policed. Why? Because they are ubiquitous. According to this perspective, policing them would be like policing cursing at bars. But is this the correct perspective? Can intrinsic conflicts of interest not be policed? Should we let them be free?

I do not think they should. Without denying their ubiquity and, thus, the difficulty of policing them, I think companies should regulate them. After all, they are as problematic as extrinsic conflicts of interest. And what does a company lose in including them in their codes of ethics? Nothing. On the contrary, the inclusion of extrinsic conflicts of interest makes it plain for all to see that exist and that they should be managed ethically as well. Their inclusion, moreover, is very simple: it only takes a good definition and a few good examples.

So, is it a blind spot or there is a deeper reason for the exclusion of this class of conflicts of interest? I think these two explanations are not mutually exclusive. But I also think that it is better to put intrinsic conflicts of interest under the spotlight in codes of ethics—even if managing them judiciously proves harder than is the case for the extrinsic kind.

ANOTHER OMISSION: WHY DO CONFLICTS OF INTEREST MATTER?

One of the main questions about conflicts of interest concerns their morally problematic nature. In this book, we have discussed this question in detail. There are several reasons why conflicts of interest are morally problematic. Perhaps the most important is that they incite us to break promises—something that is wrong in itself and tends to bring about bad consequences.

The trouble is, very few codes of ethics offer a straightforward explanation of why conflicts of interest are morally problematic and, thus, why we should manage them judiciously. Take this short example from Novartis (which is, by the way, all the company says about conflicts of interest):

> Personal interests must not influence our business judgment or decision making. Associates must disclose actual or potential conflicts of interest to their supervisor. Newly hired associates are requested to disclose any actual or potential conflicts of interest before they begin employment.[16]

While it is possible to critique the lack of an explicit definition of conflicts of interest, the quality of the implicit definition (situations in which "personal interests . . . influence our business judgment or decision making"), their typology ("actual or potential"), and the rules for their proper management ("disclose"), our focus now is on the lack of an explanation of why conflicts of interest matter. The only reason the company gives is that conflicts of interest affect "our business judgment or decision making." But why, we may ask, should we exercise caution in our business judgment or decision-making?

One might argue that the answer is obvious and that we should not expect a philosophical treatise on why conflicts of interest matter in a code of ethics. Still, just as they benefit from definitions, codes of ethics also benefit from the inclusion of clear and straightforward explanations of why they are morally problematic. I can think of two reasons why. First, because it is not uncommon to take conflicts of interest lightly when, as we already know, they deserve serious attention. Second, because to command something without offering a reason, i.e., without justifying the command, can be reasonably perceived as arbitrary. A direct explanation of why conflicts of interest matter serves to raise people's awareness in this regard, and to enhance their understanding of why the rules regarding their management—rules like evade and expose—are not mere wishes but the fruits of reason.

The best approach, then, is to explain, perhaps in an independent section or paragraph, why conflicts of interest matter, i.e., why they are morally problematic. Take the code of ethics of Johnson & Johnson—one of the few cases where an overt explanation is provided. The company directly asks why the issue matters, and this is their answer:

> The way we conduct ourselves in our business dealings impacts our reputation and the trust we maintain with stakeholders. By discouraging and avoiding conflicts of interest, we send a clear message about our loyalty to our Company's integrity and our determination to do what's right.[17]

According to Johnson & Johnson, conflicts of interest matter because when mismanaged they hurt the trust relationship between the company and the stakeholders. Had I been assigned to write this code of ethics, I would have highlighted the promise-breaking problem. Nonetheless, in its choice of wording the company still makes a strong and valid point: trust is one of the problems that comes up when discussing the problematic nature of conflicts of interest.[18] We should not, then, worry too much about coming up with a deeper reason as to why conflicts of interest matter, but to say something about this is, I think, necessary.

MANAGEMENT: INCOMPLETE MEASURES

Let's now talk about the ways codes of ethics deal with the management of conflicts of interest—and let's do it, of course, using the five "E"s of individual management: explore, evade, escape, expose, and execute.

When we review codes of ethics, we often find that the measures they highlight correspond to the second "E": evade. Take the following from Exxon Mobile Corporation:

> It is the policy of Exxon Mobile Corporation that directors, officers and employees are expected to avoid any actual or apparent conflict between

their own personal interest and the interest of the Corporation. . . . Directors, officers and employees are expected to avoid actual or apparent conflicts of interest in dealing with suppliers, customers, competitors and other third parties. Directors, officers and employees are expected to refrain from taking for themselves opportunities discovered through their use of corporate assets or through their position with the Corporation. Directors, officers, and employees are expected to avoid securities transactions based on material, non-public information learned through their positions with the Corporation. Directors, officers and employees are expected to refrain from competing with the Corporation.[19]

I can imagine the motivation behind this evade-focused policy: to send a strong message that conflicts of interest are not tolerated at all within the company. But the problem is (as we have discussed) that conflicts of interest are often unavoidable. They can arrive despite our faultlessness and even against our will. So what are Exxon Mobile Corporation employees expected to do in these situations? The company's code of ethics offers no help. Even worse, innocent employees will look guilty under this code.

Other times, codes of ethics do not mention the second "E" but instead reduce the management of conflicts of interest to the fourth "E": expose, like Netflix:

Any Netflix Party who is aware of a conflict of interest, or is concerned that a conflict might develop, is required to discuss the matter with a higher level of management or the General Counsel promptly. Senior Financial Officers may, in addition to speaking with the General Counsel, also discuss the matter with the Audit Committee.[20]

Most of the time, though, companies do include the two aforementioned "E"s. They also implicitly deal with the fifth "E": execute (our job-related duty). They do so when they say, like The Coca Cola Company does, things like "We are all expected to act in the best interest of our Company."[21] Ideally, though, codes of ethics should explicitly speak of the five "E"s, including the much neglected explore and escape.

A code of ethics would look odd if it commanded users to explore the way the company regulates conflicts of interest. Why? Because if the user is already reading the code of ethics then there is no point in saying so. What a code of ethics can do is to ask users to explore whether their particular profession or occupation regulates conflicts of interest in a more specific way—and to follow these standards. For example, people in the investment profession should consider not only the code of ethics of their employer, but, potentially, the CFA Institute's "Code of Ethics and Standards of Professional Ethics"[22] as well (which, by the way, greatly limits the management of conflicts of interest to the fourth "E": expose).

Codes of ethics, finally, should also prompt users to escape conflicts of interest, to the extent that conflicts of interest, if not avoided, can eventually and timeously be escaped—saving the need to expose.

TEXT BOX 7.3: REGULATING GIFTS AND ENTERTAINMENT

In regulating gifts and entertainment as sources of conflicts of interest, research shows that we are much more vulnerable than we think: frequent small gifts can go a long way to creating conflicts of interests and to inducing us to mismanage them. Here, I reproduce an entry from Jeff Kaplan's blog on conflicts of interest that explains this phenomenon:

> Virtually every conflict of interest policy contains monetary limits for individual acts of gift giving or entertainment, but not all seek to quantify *how many* of such acts are permitted to occur in a given time period. This issue was raised in a particularly grim way . . . by a recent study which "found that both deaths from opioid overdose and opioid prescriptions rose in areas of the country where physicians received more opioid-related marketing from pharmaceutical companies, such as consulting fees and free meals."

> Relevant to the specific issue in this post, Magdalena Cerdá, director of the Center on Opioid Epidemiology and Policy at NYU Langone Health and the senior author on the study, stated: "A lot of the discussion around the pharmaceutical industry has been around high value payments, but what seems to matter is really the number of times doctors interact with the pharmaceutical industry. . . . 'A physician's prescribing pattern could be influenced more by multiple inexpensive meals than a single high-value speaking fee', she noted."

> More generally, this finding seems to me to be significant in a broad-based way as it presumably applies to other commercial contexts as well. And, compliance officers in all industries should make sure that their COI policies address not just high-value gifts and entertainment but also high volumes of such.[23]

CONSISTENCY: "SPILLING" CONFLICTS OF INTEREST

Curiously, references in codes of ethics to the regulation of conflicts of interest sometimes escape the section devoted to conflicts of interest themselves.

Take the case of Verizon. Section 2 of the company's code of ethics, titled "Integrity and Fairness in the Workplace," regulates conflicts of interest.[24] What interests us for the moment, though, is not this but Section 4.

This section, titled "Integrity and Fairness in the Marketplace," devotes a whole section to "Gifts and Entertainments." This is the introduction:

> No gift or entertainment can be exchanged if (a) it might create the appearance of undue influence, unfairness, or impropriety, (b) it is intended to improperly influence another person's business judgment, or (c) you are participating in, conducting, or directly supervising a formal Verizon procurement process.[25]

Yet, gifts and entertainments need to be regulated because they create conflicts of interest, i.e., situations in which an interest tempts one to disregard an office- or job-related duty and that threatens the interest of someone else. Let's say you have to promote someone, change a provider, or assign a loan. If you accept a gift or entertainment from the worker, the provider, or the client before you make the decision, chances are that you will be inclined to give them what they are asking for, regardless of its merit.

When Verizon says that "no gift or entertainment can be exchanged if . . . it is intended to improperly influence another person's business judgment," they are saying, in different words, that no gift or entertainment must be exchanged if its acceptance "might impair, or even appear to impair, your [Verizon's workers] ability to make objective and fair decisions when performing your job"[26]—which takes us right back to Verizon's definition of a conflict of interest (as found in Section 2).

Let's be clear: if the goal is to regulate conflicts of interest, including the gifts and entertainment that can often create them, then Verizon is on the right path. Still, for the sake of clarity and order, the regulation of gifts and entertainment should be included within the section devoted to conflicts of interest—as, to be fair, they are in some codes of ethics.

The problem is not restricted to gifts and entertainment, as the example of Mastercard shows. The company's code of ethics regulates conflicts of interest in Section 7; it devotes a separate section to "Business Hospitality, Meals and Gifts," although most of this only addresses the improper offering of these goods and not their reception. In other words, MasterCard appears preoccupied with forbidding their workers from putting external parties in conflicts of interest. The sections I want to highlight—as instances where conflicts of interest are regulated outside the sections devoted explicitly to conflicts of interest themselves—are these: Section 8, "Anti-Corruption"; Section 10, "Related Party Transactions," and Section 14, "Political Activities."

Section 8 includes a subsection, titled simply "Conflicts of interest," that orders the following: "Avoid situations where you stand to personally benefit from a decision you made in your role at Mastercard."[27] Section 10, in turn, exhorts directors and executive officers not to "commence or continue with a related party transaction without the approval or ratification of the Board of Directors."[28] The section goes on to define "related party transaction" as a "transaction in which any 'related party' [such as a family member] had or will have a direct or indirect material interest."[29] Finally, Section 14 asks Mastercard workers to "be alert of any potential conflict of interest between your outside civil and political activities and your position at Mastercard."[30]

Again, all these aspects of conflicts of interest are better regulated than ignored. The criticism here concerns the lack of clarity and order in the way some companies go about their regulating. This, in turn, may leave some users confused. When done well, a single section should do the job.

OVERREGULATING: CONFLICTS OF INTEREST OUTSIDE CODES OF ETHICS

A final salient issue regarding the regulation of conflicts of interest, which is not necessarily a problem but can become one, is the regulation of the matter outside codes of ethics.

Citibank dedicates a substantial section of its code of ethics to conflicts of interest,[31] which deals in detail with the likes of the hiring of relatives, gifts, and entertainment, personal and related party business dealing, corporate opportunities, outside business activity, conflicts of interest with clients, customers, and counterparts, and so on.

Although it regulates conflicts of interest in detail, the code still refers users to a series of related Citibank policies: "Business, Religion and/ or Function Conflict of Interest Policies," "Employment of Relatives Policy," "City Anti-Bribery Policy," "Anti-Bribery Hiring Procedure," "Gifts and Entertainment Standard," "Employee Loan Policy," "Insider Lending Policy," "Policy on Related Party Transactions," "Outside Directorship and Business Interest Policy," and "Client Conflicts of Interest Management Policy."

A quick online search for these documents led me instead to yet another document, titled "Description of Citi's EMEA Conflicts of Interest Policy."[32] After an introduction, this document has two sections: one devoted to the identification of conflicts of interest and another to their management. When it comes to the latter, the document makes general reference to "policies and procedures ensuring fair and/or equal treatment of clients or classes of clients," "regulation of personal investment and business activities of Citi employees by Compliance," "rules governing the acceptance and granting of inducements, including disclosure of such arrangements to clients," etcetera. Now, unless Citibank is referring here to the same documents as those cited in the previous paragraph (and if they are then they should say so), the company's code of ethics appears to be sending readers to policies that, in turn, refer to other policies. The whole thing, you might agree, feels Kafkaesque. In fact, the mere act of listing the documents left me confused and overwhelmed. The problem increases when we realize that the topic of conflicts of interest is one among others in the code of ethics—i.e., when we recall that there are other ethics-related matters that employees must honor as employees of Citibank.

When we look at the other documents and policies that Citibank's code of ethics refers to, the experience worsens. On top of all these regulations, the code of ethics closes with a statement that new hires should sign in which they commit to complying with all the principles, policies, and laws outlined in the code.

In defense of Citibank, we have to consider that this is a corporation with a global presence whose economic power surpasses that of some countries. We must also recall that the financial sector is especially prone to conflicts of interest and their regulation is complex. We must consider, finally, that many of these documents may be the result of laws that compel their existence. These and other factors may explain the proliferation of regulations within the bank. Still, they should not prevent us from asking whether it is reasonable to expect employees to master conflicts of interest (and other topics) or to end up, after tackling all these documents and references, confused about the definition, classification, moral status, and management. The latter is surely not reasonable, but I am pretty it is what often transpires.

This is why, whenever possible, I favor a single, simple code of ethics that leaves matters clear, and provides the option to consult superiors or, even better, a specialized office in cases of doubt. I say "whenever possible" because, as I mentioned—with reference to Citibank—sometimes it is factors such as the scope of the company, the goods or services it offers, its worldwide presence, and the law that result in the somewhat muddled regulation of conflicts of interest.

**TEXT BOX 7.4: OTHER POLICIES MENTIONED
IN CITIBANK'S CODE OF ETHICS**

Deep breath, here goes: "Mission and Vale Propositions," "Leadership Standards," "Escalation Policy," "Global Disciplinary Review Policy," "Citi's Compensation Policy," "Business Practices Committee Charter," "Employee Handbook [for each region or country]," "Prohibition of Workplace Retaliation," "Security and Fire Safety Policy," "CSIS Security and Safety Awareness Toolkit," "City Information Technology Management Policy," "Electronic Communications Policy," "Global Social Media Policy and Guidelines," "Privacy and Confidentiality Policy," "Public Disclosure and Communications Policy," "Records Management Policy," "City Information Security Standards," "U.S. Consumer Privacy Standards (CISS)," "City Private Policy for Transferred European Workforce Data," "Fraud Risk Management Policy," "City Information Technology Management Standards," "Third Party Management Policy and Standards," "City Brand Central," "City Data Management Policy and Standards," "Records Management Policy," "City Expense Management Policy," "Initiative Expense Policy," "Code of Ethics for Financial Professionals," "Global Consumer Fairness Policy," "U.S. Fair Lending Policy," "Activities Subject to OCC Regulation 9 and Fiduciary Activities Policy and Standards," "Anti-Tying Policy," "City Standards for Suppliers," "Citi Statement of Suppliers Principles," "City Suppliers Diversity and Sustainability Program," "Insider Trading Policy," "ICG Material, Nonpublic Information Barrier Policy," "Notification Policy for Reporting Material, Nonpublic Information and Other Reportable Events," "Wall Crossing Policy and Barriers," "Personal Trading & Investment Policy," "Global AML Know Your Costumer Policy," "Global Anti-Money Laundering Policy," "Global AML Customer Identification Program," "Policy on Activities Involving U.S. Public Officials," "Anti-Boycott Policy," "Policy on Legislative Lobbying or Making Corporate Political Contributions Involving Non-U.S. Government Officials," "Anti-Boycott Policy," "Anti-Boycott Guidelines," "Global Sanctions Policy," "City Continuity of Business Policy," "Charitable Contributions Policy and Standards," "U.S. Personal Political Contributions Pre-Approval

Guide," "Environmental and Social Risk Management Policy," "Environmental and Social Policy Framework," "Sustainable Progress Strategy," "Global Citizenship website," "Citi Sustainability website," "Citi's FY2017 Modern Slavery Act Statement," and "Statement on Human Rights."[33]

CONFLICTS OF INTEREST IN CODES OF ETHICS: SOME LESSONS

This chapter may have been somewhat critical, but for a positive, constructive reason: to gather some lessons and, in so doing, to improve the regulation of conflicts of interest in codes of ethics. This section is aimed at those of you who have, or may have in the future, responsibility for rectifying, drafting, or commissioning codes of ethics.

When it comes to presenting a definition of conflicts of interest, codes of ethics should, first of all, single one out. This will give users a clear idea of what it is they are supposed to manage well. Now, in doing so, you should not get carried away: one definition is enough. In other words, you should not repeat Alibaba's mistake of including several definitions.

The inclusion of a single, singled-out definition is not enough: the definition has to be accurate. Codes must avoid mistakes such as conflating conflicts of interest with conflicting interests or providing too narrow a definition of the interests that can create conflicts of interest. Here, the definitions offered by specialists, which we have discussed in this book, come in handy. The task, then, is to look through these definitions and choose the one for their code of ethics that makes the most sense to you. All of them, generally speaking, are good (or good enough) definitions.

If codes of ethics take the opportunity to offer examples of the most-common conflicts of interest situations, they should include at least one instance of an intrinsic conflict of interest. This will make readers aware that interests inherent to the work, job, office, or position can create conflicts of interest as well.

Meanwhile, even if we all know that conflicts of interest are morally problematic and that they must therefore be managed ethically, it is a good idea to include a clear explanation of why they matter. This will, among other things, justify the rules for their proper management—as well as the corresponding sanctions for mismanaging one.

Codes of ethics must take into account the five "E"s of individual management of conflicts of interest: explore, evade, escape, expose, and execute. If a code only includes one of these, as is often the case, users may well end up confused when the chosen management measure does not actually work in a certain case. If users are encouraged to evade a conflict of interest, for instance, they will wonder what to do when they find themselves, against their will, in a conflict of interest that they were not in a position to evade in the first place. Moreover, they could even end up feeling or, even worse, being found guilty of something for which they are not to blame.

For the sake of clarity and order, codes of ethics should avoid, as far as possible, regulating conflicts of interest outside the section devoted to the topic. For instance, I do not see a strong reason to regulate the reception of gifts and entertainment in a separate section. They need to be regulated, after all, precisely because they generate conflicts of interest and not for any other reason (unless, of course, I am missing something).

Finally, you should think twice before expanding a code of ethics with references to policies external to the document. Sometimes this may be necessary, of course, but such necessity should be judged carefully. Codes of ethics are like laws; to expect anyone except lawyers to read one with enthusiasm and master their content is unrealistic and, thus, unfair. The challenge, then, is to develop a clear, short, and comprehensive regulation.

It would be nice to end this section by referring to a paradigmatic code of ethics, one that properly regulates conflicts of interest, but I am afraid I have not been able to find one. Each code has its own strengths and weaknesses—without denying, of course, that (like everything else) some codes are better than others.

CHAPTER SUMMARY

In this chapter, I evaluated the way conflicts of interest are regulated in codes of ethics, with (despite appearances) a constructive goal: to prepare the ground for improvements to these codes.

In the first section, I focused on how codes of ethics define conflicts of interest and the several ways in which codes of ethics can miss the target. One mistake is to simply omit a definition altogether, or at least not to single it out, like in the case of Nestlé's code of ethics.

Another error is to include a definition, but a flawed one. The most common such error is to conflate conflicts of interest with conflicting interests, of which Microsoft's code of ethics is a good example. We know, though, that not every conflicting interest is a conflict of interest.

A third error regarding definitions is to include several definitions. As an example, I discussed Alibaba's code of ethics, which includes no fewer than three definitions of conflicts of interest.

In the same section, I also signaled a fourth way that codes of ethics can err with regard to definitions: providing narrow definitions of the interests that can cause conflicts of interest. Here, I offered three examples: Alphabet, Microsoft, and Pfizer.

I devoted the third section to pointing out how, with reference to examples of typical conflicts of interest, companies tend to focus exclusively on extrinsic conflicts of interest—bypassing entirely the extremely common and equally problematic intrinsic class. Cisco and Chevron served as illustrations.

Then, in the fourth section, I pointed out how most codes of ethics do not bother explaining why conflicts of interest are morally problematic. Novartis's code of ethics came in handy by way of demonstration, and by way of contrast with that of Johnson & Johnson—one of the few cases in which a code of ethics explains why we should treat conflicts of interest with care.

I explained, in the fifth section, how codes of ethics also err in the way they regulate the management of conflicts of interest. This often occurs through a flat command to simply evade them, like in the case of Exxon Mobile Corporation, even though not all conflicts of interest are evadable. Netflix's code, in turn, is an instance of one that commands only to expose conflicts of interest. But these are just two of the five "E"s of individual management. The Coca Cola Company, finally, illustrated how the fifth "E": execute, is often, to some degree, present. But there is no code that deals with all the "Es," apparently.

In the sixth section, I highlighted how codes of ethics sometimes approach the regulation of conflicts of interest outside the section devoted to conflicts of interest themselves. The cases of Verizon and Mastercard illustrated this point well.

The seventh section I dedicated to explaining how codes of ethics occasionally send readers to external documents where conflicts of interest are further regulated. In the case of Citibank, this was taken to an extreme, referring readers to a very long list of external policies and regulations.

Finally, in the eighth section, I summed up some lessons from the review with a view to improving the regulation of conflicts of interest in codes of ethics—again, so that readers with the power to rectify, draft, or commission a code of ethics do not make these same mistakes.

Through several notes, I discussed the dubious impact of codes of ethics, how to regulate intrinsic conflicts of interest, and how vulnerable we are in terms of gifts and entertainment.

All this opens up the debate around codes of ethics in general, and not just around their treatment of conflicts of interest. My view is that codes of ethics need to be rethought, but exactly how and why transcends the scope of this book.

QUESTIONS AND EXERCISES FOR REFLECTION

Grab the code of ethics of the organization where you study or work. Alternatively, look for the code of ethics of your current or future profession. If you are still unable to identify a code of ethics that applies to you, grab a code of ethics at random and answer the following questions:

1. Does it define conflicts of interest properly? Or do you find any of the problems signaled in this chapter?
2. Does it focus exclusively on extrinsic conflicts of interest?
3. Does the code explain why conflicts of interest are morally problematic—directly or at least indirectly?
4. Does the code regulate the management of conflicts of interest in a comprehensible manner? What does it say exactly?
5. Does the code regulate conflicts of interest outside the section devoted to conflicts of interest? Or is it all contained in the section?
6. Does the code refer users to more external regulations and policies regarding conflicts of interest?
7. How does your code regulate gifts and entertainment? Through a flat prohibition or through certain limitations?
8. In general, how do you feel about the code? Does it need any improvement?
9. How do you feel about codes of ethics in general?
10. Have I missed any mistakes that you have noticed codes of ethics commonly make when regulating conflicts of interest?

CONCLUSION

As the title promised, this book has served as an introduction to the ethics of conflicts of interest in business. Let's briefly summarize, by way of conclusion, some of the main lessons from each chapter and see, with greater clarity, how the chapters fit together.

In the first chapter, I introduced ethics with reference to its supreme, although somewhat neglected, principle: the moral law. More specifically, I focused on two of its most influential versions: the categorical imperative, from Kant's deontology and the principle of utility, from Mill's utilitarianism. According to Kant, the moral law is grounded in reason and orders to act in accordance with maxims or personal principles that we would support to become universal law. From another angle, it orders that we treat humanity, in ourselves and in others, always as an end and never as a mere means. According to Mill, on the other hand, the moral law is grounded in happiness, defined as pleasure, and orders that we promote the greatest amount of it for the greatest number of people. For both, the moral law is the source of more concrete, secondary moral duties such as "do not kill," "do not steal," "keep your promises," etcetera. Both also see moral problems as situations in which an interest tempts us to disregard a moral duty.

In chapter 2, devoted to business ethics, I focused on the most common way of speaking of it: corporate social responsibility. In so doing, I offered, side by side, two rival positions: Friedman's shareholder theory and Freeman's stakeholder theory. According to Friedman, the social responsibility of *business executives* (remember how he focuses on individuals) is to materialize shareholder's wishes, which is usually to make money—within the limits of law and ethics. Friedman criticizes CSR for the following reason: it means business executives breaking their duty to their employers, the shareholders. Freeman's stakeholder theory, on the other hand, offers a critique of the shareholder theory and a defense of, well, his own stakeholder theory. He argues that the former is unsound, in part, because of a responsibility principle that compels *businesses* to adopt stakeholder theory, i.e., to consider the interests of all stakeholders in everything they do. Freeman grounds this responsibility principle in several moral theories, including the ones introduced in chapter 1. In the same chapter, I then analyze what both the shareholder and the stakeholder theories have to say about conflicts of interest, which, surprisingly, is not much—I say "surprisingly" to the extent that conflicts of interest are at the heart of business ethics. Finally, I conclude the chapter by presenting a criticism of both theories for their elitism, i.e., for appealing to business executives and business owners, and not to all workers. It is precisely this sort of elitism that justifies a departure in business ethics from corporate social responsibility to conflicts of interest.

I devoted the remaining chapters to conflicts of interest. These chapters would not have been possible—and I am not exaggerating a little bit—without the contributions of authors such as Davis, Luebke, Boatright, Carson, Stark, and so on, who have analyzed conflicts of interest philosophically. For the most part, I have organized their contributions, analyzed them, and, finally, take a position. There have been, of course, moments of originality in these chapters, but let's not forget the main purpose of the book, as established by its title: to introduce readers to the ethics of conflicts of interest in business. (That said, chapter 7—"Conflicts of Interest in Codes of Ethics"—is, as far as I am aware, the first in its kind.)

In chapter 3, I dealt with the preliminary question regarding conflicts of interest: What are they? How should we define them? Inspired by Socrates and Plato, I first considered how definitions work, how they can fail, and how the use of examples serves the whole enterprise of defining things. I then considered and criticized the definition of conflicts of interest as conflicting interests. My next step was to "x-ray" a good example of a conflict of interest. This revealed the presence of a duty, and not only of interests, in all conflicts of interest. I then came to a preliminary definition: a conflict of interest is a situation in which an interest temps one to disregard a duty—a situation that threatens the interest of someone else. The challenge from here was to determine what kind of duty and what kind of interest make conflicts of interest special, differentiating them from ordinary moral problems. After pondering the insights of some of the cited authors, I took a position and defined conflicts of interest as a situation in which a (tangible or intangible interest) tempts one to disregard an office-, position-, work-, or job-related duty—a situation that threatens the interest of someone else.

Then, in chapter 4, I classified conflicts of interest into formal and informal, potential and actual, real and apparent, individual and organizational, and extrinsic and intrinsic varieties. I also considered the subtypes of intrinsic conflicts of interest: "many principals, one duty" and "many duties, one principal." Finally, I discussed the subtypes of the "many duties, one principal" type of conflicts of interest: those that involve duties to diagnose and to serve, and those that involve duties to judge and to advocate. In between, I paid special attention to the question of whether organizations per se can have conflicts of interest, considering that they are not, properly speaking, moral agents.

I devoted the fifth chapter to the assessment of conflicts of interest: why are they morally problematic if they involve position- or job-related duties rather than moral ones? As a preliminary step, I explained, as scholars agree but businesspeople sometimes forget, how conflicts of interest are not wrong in themselves. In short, they are moral problems, not mismanaged moral problems. But why, again, are they problematic? Ultimately, because they move us to break promises. The burden of the chapter was, then, to derive, from the moral law in its deontological and utilitarian versions, the moral duty to keep promises. The deontological derivation is based on the categorical imperative in both the formula of universal law and the formula of humanity. The utilitarian derivation, in turn, is based on two interpretations of the principle of utility: those of act and rule utilitarianism. Just as all roads lead to Rome, both derivations led to the moral duty to keep promises. In short, breaking promises is wrong both in itself (deontological argument) and because of the consequences (utilitarian argument). Focusing on the latter, I then called upon readers to ponder the importance of what they do (or will do) for a living. Even the humblest job and job-related duty, I argued, can have extraordinary consequences if managed irresponsibly. Then I concluded the chapter by gathering additional reasons that explain the morally problematic nature of conflicts of interest.

In chapter 6, I covered the proper management of conflicts of interest. I considered two levels of management: individual and organizational. With regard to the former, I introduced the five "E"s of individual management: explore, evade, escape, expose, and execute. First, explore the way your organization, occupation, profession, or whatever regulates conflicts of interest. Then evade, escape, and expose the conflicts of interest you find on the road. Finally, execute your work-related duty. When it came to the latter, I introduced the ABC of organizational management: align, build walls, and codify. First, align the interests of the members of the organization with the interest of those whom they serve. Second, build ethical walls between units or teams, so they do not share information that might generate conflicts of interest. Third, codify conflicts of interest. In connection to this third point, I said some words about the history, the justification, and the most common content of codes of ethics—as one of the most common means of regulating conflicts of interest. This, in turn, opened the door for the next and final chapter, devoted to an analysis of conflicts of interest in codes of ethics.

That is, in chapter 7, I analyzed the way business codes of ethics regulate conflicts of interest. More specifically, I signaled several ways in which codes of ethics tend to err when regulating them. First, they err regarding their definition. For instance, codes of ethics sometimes simply omit definitions, leaving users uncertain about what they are supposed to manage properly. Or if do they include a definition, they are often flawed. For instance, some codes of ethics conflate conflicts of interest with conflicting interests. Other times, they define interests too narrowly. Some codes of ethics even include multiple incompatible definitions. Second, codes of ethics can err regarding the classification of conflicts of interest. The most common mistake here is to refer exclusively to the extrinsic type, as if intrinsic conflicts of interest did not exist, were not morally problematic, or were impossible to regulate. Third, codes of ethics often say nothing about the morally problematic nature of conflicts of interest. In other words, they do not explain why they need to be properly managed in the first place. Fourth, codes of ethics almost never include all the options available to manage them ethically at the individual level. To mention one example, sometimes the only thing we find are flat commands to evade them, as if all conflicts of interest were evadable. Fifth, codes of ethics sometimes regulate conflicts of interest outside the section specifically devoted to conflicts of interest, which can be confusing to users. Sixth and finally, codes of ethics can overregulate conflicts of interest by referring users to external documents that end up overwhelming everybody (except, perhaps, lawyers). This done, I concluded the chapter by gathering lessons for those with the power—or who may have the power in the future—to rectify, draft, or commission codes of ethics.

You may disagree with one or more of the positions taken in this book. That is perfectly fine, even desirable, if you see things better than the book—that is, than me. But if after reading this book you have gained a better understanding of ethics, business ethics, and, specially, of conflicts of interest, the book will have accomplished its goal.

NOTES

INTRODUCTION

1. https://www.businesswire.com/news/home/20170615005558/en/Eaten
-Reality-Sandwich-Put-Ducks-Row-Not.

2. https://www.bbc.com/news/business-48760790.

CHAPTER 1

1. I. Kant, *Grounding for the Metaphysics of Morals*, trans. J. W. Elllington, third edition (Indianapolis: Hackett, 1993), 4:412.

2. Kant, *Grounding for the Metaphysics of Morals*, 4:432.

3. As quoted by William Stigand in *The Life, Work, and Opinions of Heinrich Heine*, vol. 1 (London: Longmans, Green Co., 1875), 429.

4. Kant, *Grounding for the Metaphysics of Morals*, 4: 421.

5. Kant, *Grounding for the Metaphysics of Morals*, 4:400, footnote 13.

6. Kant, *Grounding for the Metaphysics of Morals*, 4:424.

7. Kant, *Grounding for the Metaphysics of Morals*, 4:429.

8. J. S. Mill, *Utilitarianism (and the 1868 Speech on Capital Punishment)*, second edition, ed. G. Sher (Indianapolis: Hackett Publishing Company [1861 and 1868] 2001), 7.

9. Mill, *Utilitarianism (and the 1868 Speech on Capital Punishment)*, 7.

10. Mill, *Utilitarianism (and the 1868 Speech on Capital Punishment)*, 8.

11. Mill, *Utilitarianism (and the 1868 Speech on Capital Punishment)*, 23.

12. Mill, *Utilitarianism (and the 1868 Speech on Capital Punishment)*, 22.

13. R. Crisp, *Mill On Utilitarianism* (London and New York: Routledge, 2001), 7.

14. Crisp, *Mill On Utilitarianism*, 2.

15. Mill, *Utilitarianism (and the 1868 Speech on Capital Punishment)*, 35–36, 39.

16. Mill, *Utilitarianism (and the 1868 Speech on Capital Punishment)*, 36–37.

17. Mill, *Utilitarianism (and the 1868 Speech on Capital Punishment)*, 38.

18. Mill, *Utilitarianism (and the 1868 Speech on Capital Punishment)*, 39.

19. Kant, *Grounding for the Metaphysics of Morals*, 4:402.

20. Kant, *Grounding for the Metaphysics of Morals*, 4:405.

21. Kant, *Grounding for the Metaphysics of Morals*, 4:435.

22. Kant, *Grounding for the Metaphysics of Morals*, 4:440.

23. Kant, *Grounding for the Metaphysics of Morals*, 4:442.

24. Kant, *Grounding for the Metaphysics of Morals*, 4:418.

25. I. Kant, "Critique of Practical Reason," in *Immanuel Kant: Practical Philosophy*, trans. and ed. M. J. Gregor (Cambridge: Cambridge University Press, 2015), 5:517.

26. Kant, "Critique of Practical Reason," 5:130.

27. For more on this, see Victoria S. Wike's book *Kant on Happiness in Ethics* (New York: SUNY Press, 1994).

28. www.effectivealtruism.com.

29. P. Singer, *The Life You Can Save* (New York: Random House, 2010). See also: www.thelifeyoucansave.org.

30. W. MacAskill, *Doing Good Better* (New York: Penguin Random House, 2015).

31. www.givewell.org.

32. www.animalcharityevaluators.org.

33. J. S. Mill, "The Subjection of Women," in *On Liberty and Other Essays*, ed. J. Gray (Oxford: Oxford University Press [1859] 1991), 469–582.

34. Mill defended capital punishment with the argument that it is dissuasive in his "1868 Speech on Capital Punishment." See *Utilitarianism and the 1868 Speech on Capital Punishment*, 65–71.

35. For more on this, see https://ethicsofsuicide.lib.utah.edu/selections/john-stuart-mill/.

36. J. S. Mill, "On Liberty," in *On Liberty and Other Essays*, ed. J. Gray (Oxford: Oxford University Press [1859] 1991), 5.

37. Mill, "On Liberty," 14.

38. Mill, "On Liberty," 15.

39. Mill, "On Liberty," 59.

40. Kant, *Grounding for the Metaphysics of Morals*, 4:422.

41. Kant, *Grounding for the Metaphysics of Morals*, 4:422.

42. Kant, *Grounding for the Metaphysics of Morals*, 4:423.

43. Kant, *Grounding for the Metaphysics of Morals*, 4:423.

44. Kant, *Grounding for the Metaphysics of Morals*, 4:405.

45. Mill, *Utilitarianism (and the 1868 Speech on Capital Punishment)*, 17.

46. Mill, *Utilitarianism (and the 1868 Speech on Capital Punishment)*, 17.

CHAPTER 2

1.   Aristotle, *Metaphysics*, trans. Hippocrates G. Apostle (Des Moines: The Peripatetic Press [350 B.C.E.] 1979), 1003a33.

2.   M. Friedman, "The Social Responsibility of Business Is to Increase its Profits," in *Ethical Theory and Business*, ninth edition, eds. D. G. Arnold, T. L. Beauchamp, and N. E. Bowie (Boston: Pearson, 2013), 53. Original version available online at https://graphics8.nytimes.com/packages/pdf/business/miltonfr iedman1970.pdf.

3.   Friedman, "The Social Responsibility of Business is to Increase its Profits," 54.

4.   P. Kottler and N. Lee, *Corporate Social Responsibility: Doing the Most Good for Your Company and Your Cause* (Hoboken, NJ: John Wiley Sons, 2005), 10–11.

5.   Friedman, "The Social Responsibility of Business is to Increase its Profits," 55.

6.   Friedman, "The Social Responsibility of Business is to Increase its Profits," 55.

7.   https://www.bbc.com/news/stories-51332811.

8.   https://mynorthwest.com/1701240/washington-state-head-tax-bill-hearing/.

9.   https://scocal.stanford.edu/opinion/greenman-v-yuba-power-products -inc-27186.

10.   https://www.nlrb.gov/how-we-work/national-labor-relations-act.

11.   https://www.eeoc.gov/laws/statutes/adea.cfm.

12.   Of course, this is debatable. Nothing guarantees that legislation will keep moving in this direction. For instance, there is nothing to prevent the world from being ruled by libertarians who would reverse the trend.

13.   R. E. Freeman, "Managing for Stakeholders," in *Ethical Theory and Business*, ninth edition, eds. D. G. Arnold, T. L. Beauchamp, and N. E. Bowie (Boston: Pearson, 2013), 60.

14.   Freeman, "Managing for Stakeholders," 60.

15.   Freeman, "Managing for Stakeholders," 61.

16.   Freeman, "Managing for Stakeholders," 64.

17.   Freeman, "Managing for Stakeholders," 64.

18.   Freeman, "Managing for Stakeholders," 65.

19.   Freeman, "Managing for Stakeholders," 66.

20.   Freeman, "Managing for Stakeholders," 66.

21.   G. Pence, *A Dictionary of Common Philosophical Terms* (New York: The McGraw-Hill Companies, 2000), 43.

22.   Freeman, "Managing for Stakeholders," 66.

23.   Friedman, "The Social Responsibility of Business is to Increase its Profits," 53.

24.   Kottler and Lee, *Corporate Social Responsibility: Doing the Most Good for Your Company and Your Cause*, 23–24.

25. We will discuss this later, in chapter 4.
26. Freeman, "Managing for Stakeholders," 60.
27. Freeman, "Managing for Stakeholders," 64.
28. Freeman, "Managing for Stakeholders," 62.
29. Freeman, "Managing for Stakeholders," 64.
30. Thomas L. Carson would dispute this. He says that not all conflicts of interest involve self-dealing. For instance, serving a friend is not self-dealing—it is serving someone else. To the extent that one has an interest in serving the friends' interest, though, I think we can say that, loosely speaking, all conflicts of interest involve self-dealing. For more on this, see Thomas Carson, "Conflicts of Interest and Self-Dealing in the Professions: A Review Essay," *Business Ethics Quarterly* 14, no. 1 (2004): 168–169.
31. Existential philosopher Søren Kierkegaard (Denmark–Norway 1813–1855) speaks of three (progressive) stages of life: the aesthetic, the ethical, and the religious. S. Kierkegaard, *Either/Or: A Fragment of Life*, trans. Alastair Hannay (London: Penguin Books, 1992).
32. Friedman, "The Social Responsibility of Business is to Increase its Profits," 55.
33. D. Melé, "Corporate Social Responsibility Theories," in *The Oxford Handbook of Corporate Social Responsibility*, eds. A. Crane, A. McWilliams, D. Matten, J. Moon, and D. S. Stegel (Oxford: Oxford University Press, 2008), 55–62.
34. Freeman, "Managing for Stakeholders," 66.
35. Melé, "Corporate Social Responsibility Theories," 63.
36. Melé, "Corporate Social Responsibility Theories," 49–55 and 68–75.
37. Freeman, "Managing for Stakeholders," 57.
38. https://dictionary.cambridge.org/dictionary/english/executive.
39. Friedman, "The Social Responsibility of Business is to Increase its Profits," 53.
40. Carson, "Conflicts of Interest and Self-Dealing in the Professions: A Review Essay," 179.

CHAPTER 3

1. https://www.merriam-webster.com/dictionary/table.
2. Plato, *Five Dialogues. Euthyphro, Apology, Crito, Meno, Phaedo*, trans. G. M. A. Grupe and rev. by J. M. Cooper (Indianapolis, IN: Hackett, 2002), 5e-d.
3. Plato, *Eutyphro*, 6d.
4. Plato, *Republic*, trans. A. Bloom (New York: Basic Books [380 BC] 1991), 331e.
5. Plato, *Republic*, 331e.
6. M. Davis, "Conflicts of Interest," *Business and Professional Ethics Journal* 1, no. 4 (1982): 21.

7. M. Davis, "Conflict of Interest," in *Encyclopedia of Applied Ethics*, vol. 1, second edition, eds. R. Chadwick, D. Callahan and P. Singer (Amsterdam: Elsevier, 2012), 571.

8. T. Carson, "Conflicts of Interest and Self-Dealing in the Professions: A Review Essay," *Business Ethics Quarterly* 14, no. 1 (2004): 162.

9. N. R. Luebke, "Conflict of Interest as a Moral Category," *Business and Professional Ethics Journal* 6, no.1 (1987): 68.

10. One may argue that this is not an instance of a fiduciary relationship, i.e., that "fiduciary" is being interpreted too broadly. Consider, though, this clarification from the Merriam-Webster dictionary: "Fiduciary relationships often concern money, but the word *fiduciary* does not, in and of itself, suggest financial matters. Rather, *fiduciary* applies to any situation in which one person justifiably places confidence and trust in someone else and seeks that person's help or advice in some matter. The attorney-client relationship is a fiduciary one, for example, because the client trusts the attorney to act in the best interest of the client at all times. *Fiduciary* can also be used as a noun for the person who acts in a fiduciary capacity, and *fiduciarily* or *fiducially* can be called upon if you are in need of an adverb. The words are all faithful to their origin: Latin *fidere,* which means 'to trust.'" https://www.merriam-webster.com/dictionary/fiduciary.

11. J. Boatright, "Conflict of Interest," in *Encyclopedia of Business Ethics and Society*, vol. 1, ed. R. W. Kolb (Los Angeles: SAGE Publications, 2008), 400.

12. Boatright, "Conflicts of Interest," 400.

13. Carson, "Conflicts of Interest and Self-Dealing in the Professions," 165.

14. Perhaps office- and position-related duties include duties other than work- or job-related ones. Again, I am using the term "job duties" for the sake of clarity. The vast majority of conflicts of interest, in any case, involve these kinds of duties.

15. Davis, "Conflicts of Interest": 22.

16. A. P. Schwab, "Defining Conflicts of Interest in Terms of Judgment," *Business and Professional Ethics Journal* 38, no. 1 (2019): 122.

17. Another question is: Why does Schwab bypass Carson's contributions to the debate? In fact, Carson is not even mentioned by Schwab—even though Carson is one of the towering figures in the discussion around conflicts of interest.

18. Luebke, "Conflict of Interest as a Moral Category," 69.

19. Davis, "Conflict of Interest," 23.

20. Luebke, "Conflict of Interest as a Moral Category," 74.

21. Boatright, "Conflict of Interest: An Agency Analysis," in *Ethics and Agency Theory*, eds. N. Bowie and R. E. Freeman (Oxford: Oxford University Press, 1992), 192.

22. Boatright, "Conflict of Interest," 400.

23. Boatright, "Conflict of Interest," 400.

24. https://www.merriam-webster.com/dictionary/interest.

25. https://www.merriam-webster.com/dictionary/tangible.

26. Carson, "Conflicts of Interest," 388.

27.   Carson, "Conflicts of Interest," 388.

28.   For another discussion of the definition of conflicts of interest (and of their moral status), see my article "Conflicts of Interest: A Moral Analysis," *Business Professional Ethics Journal* 39, no. 1 (2020): 121–142. Also, for a response to my article that, in addition, analyses conflicts of interest from a Rawlsian perspective, look for the forthcoming paper by Franklin Ibañez, "A Necessary Ethics Definition for Conflicts of Interest" (working title), *Business Professional Ethics Journal* (forthcoming).

CHAPTER 4

1.   Aristotle's full definition, classification, etcetera of virtue is found in book 2 of his *Nicomachean Ethics*, trans. J. Sachs (Newburyport, MA: Focus Publishing, 2011).

2.   M. Davis, "Conflicts of Interest," *Business and Professional Ethics Journal* 1, no. 4 (1982): 22.

3.   M. Davis, "Conflicts of Interest Revisited," *Business and Professional Ethics Journal* 12, no. 4 (1993): 23–24.

4.   N. R. Luebke, "Conflict of Interest as a Moral Category," *Business and Professional Ethics Journal* 6, no. 1 (1987): 74.

5.   M. Davis, "Conflict of Interest," in *Encyclopedia of Applied Ethics*, vol. 1., second edition, eds. R. Chadwick, D. Callahan, and P. Singer (Amsterdam: Elsevier, 2012), 575.

6.   N. R. Luebke, "Conflict of Interest as a Moral Category," *Business Professional Ethics Journal* 6, no. 1 (1987): 72.

7.   Davis, "Conflict of Interest," 576.

8.   A. Stark, "Comparing Conflicts of Interest Across the Professions," in *Conflict of Interest in the Professions*, eds. M. Davis and A. Stark (Oxford: Oxford University Press, 2001), 348–349 (note 1). The M. Pritchard text cited therein is "Conflicts of Interest: Conceptual and Normative Issues," *Academic Medicine* 12, no. 71 (1996).

9.   Luebke, "Conflict of Interest as a Moral Category," 68.

10.   T. Carson, "Conflicts of Interest," *Journal of Business Ethics* 13, no. 5 (1994): 389.

11.   A. P. Schwab, "Defining Conflicts of Interest in Terms of Judgment," *Business and Professional Ethics Journal* 38, no. 1 (2019): 111.

12.   J. Boatright, "Conflict of Interest: An Agency Analysis," in *Ethics and Agency Theory*, eds. N. Bowie and R. E. Freeman (Oxford: Oxford University Press, 1992), 191–192.

13.   Boatright, "Conflict of Interest: An Agency Analysis," 194.

14.   See, for instance, N. E. Bowie, *Business Ethics: A Kantian Perspective* (Massachusetts: Blackwell, 1999).

15.   M. C. Altman, "The Decomposition of the Corporate Body: What Kant Cannot Contribute to Business Ethics," *Journal of Business Ethics* 74, no. 3 (2007): 253. 335–351

16.   A. Stark, "Comparing Conflicts of Interest Across the Professions," in *Conflict of Interest in the Professions*, eds. by M. Davis and A. Stark (Oxford: Oxford University Press, 2001), 336.

17.   Stark, "Comparing Conflicts of Interest Across the Professions," 336.

18.   Stark, "Comparing Conflicts of Interest Across the Professions," 336.

19.   Stark, "Comparing Conflicts of Interest Across the Professions," 335.

20.   Stark, "Comparing Conflicts of Interest Across the Professions," 336.

21.   T. Carson, "Conflicts of Interest and Self-Dealing in the Professions," *Business Ethics Quarterly* 14, no. 1 (2004): 175.

22.   Stark, "Comparing Conflicts of Interest Across the Professions," 336.

23.   This topic will be addressed in chapter 7.

CHAPTER 5

1.   F. Nietzsche, *On the Genealogy of Morals*, trans. D. Smith (Oxford: Oxford University Press, 2008), 1:7.

2.   T. Carson, "Conflicts of Interest and Self-Dealing in the Professions: A Review Essay," *Business Ethics Quarterly* 14, no. 1 (2004): 167.

3.   I. Kant, *Grounding for the Metaphysics of Morals*, trans. J. W. Ellington, third edition (Indianapolis, IN: Hackett, 1993), 421.

4.   Kant, *Grounding for the Metaphysics of Morals*, 4:429.

5.   Kant, *Grounding for the Metaphysics of Morals*, 4:430.

6.   Bernd-Jurgen Brandes had a hand in exactly this; he was the cannibal. Michael Sandel tells and reflects on the story in *Justice: What's the Right Thing to Do?* (New York: Farrar, Straus and Giroux, 2009), 73–74.

7.   For this and more fascinating cases, see M. Sandel, *What Money Can't Buy: The Moral Limits of Markets* (New York: Farrar, Straus and Giroux, 2012).

8.   This piece by A. A. Newman in *The New York Times* explains how this works: https://www.nytimes.com/2009/02/18/business/media/18adco.html.

9.   Kant, *Grounding for the Metaphysics of Morals*, 4:429.

10.   For more on this debate, see R. Crisp, *Mill on Utilitarianism* (London: Routledge, 2001), 102–112.

11.   J. S. Mill, *Utilitarianism (and the 1868 Speech on Capital Punishment)*, second edition (Indianapolis, IN: Hackett, 2001), 15.

12.   Mill, *Utilitarianism (and the 1868 Speech on Capital Punishment)*, 17.

13.   Mill, *Utilitarianism (and the 1868 Speech on Capital Punishment)*, 19.

14.   www.effectivealtruism.org.

15.   For a good overview of this and other moral duties in different cultures and religions throughout history, see "Illustrations of the Tao," by C. S. Lewis, which is

contained as an appendix of *The Abolition of Man* (New York: HarperOne, 2000), 83–101.

16. https://www.nbc.com/the-office.

17. https://www.worldbank.org/en/topic/governance/brief/anti-corruption.

18. Carson, "Conflicts of Interest and Self-Dealing in the Professions: A Review Essay," 168.

19. M. Davis, "Conflict of Interest," in *Encyclopedia of Applied Ethics*, vol. 1, second edition, eds. R. Chadwick, D. Callahan and P. Singer (Amsterdam: Elsevier, 2012), 573.

20. N. R. Luebke, "Conflict of Interest as a Moral Category," *Business and Professional Ethics Journal* 6, no. 1 (1987): 72.

21. J. Boatright, "Conflict of Interest," in *Encyclopedia of Business Ethics and Society*, vol. 1, ed. R. W. Kolb (Thousand Oaks, CA: SAGE Publications, 2008), 401.

CHAPTER 6

1. J. Boatright, "Conflict of Interest," in *Encyclopedia of Business Ethics and Society*, vol. 1, ed. R. W. Kolb (Thousand Oaks, CA: SAGE Publications, 2008), 402–403.

2. Boatright, "Conflict of Interest," 403.

3. Bank of America, "Code of Ethics," personal archives, 5. After this book was written, the Code has been actualized and allows gifts with certain restrictions: https://tinyurl.com/4rbc8y.

4. JP Morgan Chase, "Code of Conduct 2019," personal archives, 27-28.

5. W. Norman and C. MacDonald, "Conflicts of Interest," in *The Oxford Handbook of Business Ethics*, eds. G. G. Brenkert, and Tom L. Beauchamp (New York: Oxford University Press, 2010), 452.

6. M. Davis, "Conflict of Interest," in *Encyclopedia of Applied Ethics*, vol. 1, second edition, eds. R. Chadwick, D. Callahan and P. Singer (Amsterdam: Elservier, 2012), 574.

7. M. Davis, "Introduction," in *Conflicts of Interest in the Professions*, eds. M. Davis and A. Stark (Oxford: Oxford University Press, 2001), 12.

8. N. R. Luebke, "Conflict of Interest as a Moral Category," *Business and Professional Ethics Journal* 6, no. 1 (1987): 71.

9. T. Carson, "Conflicts of Interest," *Journal of Business Ethics* 13, no. 5 (1994): 396.

10. Davis, "Conflict of Interest," 575.

11. Luebke, "Conflict of Interest as a Moral Category," 72.

12. Davis, "Conflict of Interest," 574–575.

13. D. M. Cain, G. Loewenstein, and D. A. Moore, "Coming Clean but Playing Dirtier: The Shortcomings of Disclosure as a Solution to Conflicts of

Interest," in *Conflicts of Interest: Challenges and Solutions in Business, Law, Medicine, and Public Policy*, eds. D. A. Moore, D. M. Cain, G. Loewenstein, and M. H. Bazerman (New York: Cambridge University Press, 2005).

14.   W. Norman and C. MacDonald, "Conflicts of Interest," in *The Oxford Handbook of Business Ethics*, eds. G. G. Brenkert, and Tom L. Beauchamp (New York: Oxford University Press, 2010), 458.

15.   I. Kant, *Grounding for the Metaphysics of Morals*, trans. J. W. Elllington, third edition (Indianapolis, IN: Hackett, 1993), 4:420.

16.   Boatright, "Conflict of Interest," 402.

17.   Boatright, "Conflict of Interest," 402.

18.   https://www.epi.org/publication/ceo-compensation-2018/.

19.   T. Carson, "Conflicts of Interest and Self-Dealing in the Professions: A Review Essay," *Business Ethics Quarterly* 14, no. 1 (2004): 179.

20.   *A Dictionary of Finance and Banking* (Oxford: Oxford University Press, 1998), 81.

21.   Boatright, "Conflict of Interest," 403.

22.   https://law.justia.com/cases/california/court-of-appeal/3d/200/272.html.

23.   See, for instance, M. Kaptein and M. S. Schwartz, "The Effectiveness of Business Codes: A Critical Examination of Existing Studies and the Development of an Integrated Research Model," *Journal of Business Ethics* 77 (2008): 111–127.

24.   G. C. S. Benson, "Codes of Ethics," *Journal of Business Ethics* 8, no. 5 (1989): 305–319.

25.   Benson, "Codes of Ethics," 312.

CHAPTER 7

1.   Companies name their codes of ethics in different ways: code of conduct, code of business conduct and ethics, code of business conduct, etcetera. Here, we will just use "code of ethics."

2.   Alphabet, "Code of Conduct," https://tinyurl.com/y2bg6hyx, accessed April 20, 2020.

3.   JP Morgan Chase, "Code of Conduct 2019," personal archives, 23.

4.   Nestlé, "Code of Business Conduct," https://tinyurl.com/ycpqqr48, accessed April 20, 2020, 2.

5.   Alibaba Group, "Code of Ethics," https://tinyurl.com/yc2zb5hv, accessed April 20, 2020, 2.

6.   M. Kaptein and M. S. Schwartz, "The Effectiveness of Business Codes: A Critical Examination of Existing Studies and the Development of an Integrated Research Model," *Journal of Business Ethics* 77 (2008): 122.

7.   Alphabet, "Code of Conduct," https://tinyurl.com/y2bg6hyx, accessed April 20, 2020.

8.   Microsoft, "Standards of Business Conduct," https://www.microsoft.com/en-us/legal/compliance, accessed May 11, 2021, 38.

9.   Pfizer, "The Blue Book: Summary of Pfizer Policies on Business Conduct," https://tinyurl.com/ybfyg948, accessed April 20, 2020, 28.

10.   T. Carson, "Conflicts of Interest," *Journal of Business Ethics* 13, no. 5 (1994): 388.

11.   Cisco, "2019 Code of Business Conduct," https://tinyurl.com/y8bymchp, accessed April 21, 2020, 18.

12.   Cisco, "2019 Code of Business Conduct," 18.

13.   Cisco, "2019 Code of Business Conduct," 19.

14.   Chevron, "Business Conduct and Ethics Code," https://tinyurl.com/255bx2ry, accessed April 21, 2020, 12.

15.   A. Stark, "Comparing Conflict of Interest Across the Professions," in *Conflict of Interest in the Professions*, eds. M. Davis and A. Stark (Oxford: Oxford University Press, 2001), 335–351.

16.   Novartis, "Code of Conduct," https://tinyurl.com/y8bymchp, accessed April 21, 2020, 5. After this book was written, the Code has been actualized and specifies why conflicts of interest matter: https://tinyurl.com/rd4vhyvk.

17.   Johnson and Johnson, "Code of Business Conduct," https://tinyurl.com/y8wkwc5g, accessed April 21, 2020, 30.

18.   Luebke, for instance, says the following: "Since one seldom leaves a CI without loss or curtailment of the fiduciary relationship, it is generally wrong knowingly to enter or knowingly to fail to avoid a CI. This prescription is similar to that against promising with the intent of non-performance; it is not only destructive of the given instance of trust but is [it] also contributes to a milieu of distrust." N. R. Luebke, "Conflict of Interest as a Moral Category," *Business and Professional Ethics Journal* 6, no. 1 (1987): 70.

19.   Exxon Mobile Corporation, "Code of Ethics," https://tinyurl.com/ycrqf9v8, accessed April 21, 2020, 5.

20.   Netflix, "Code of Ethics," https://tinyurl.com/ycgqv88r, accessed April 21, 2020, 1.

21.   The Coca-Cola Company, "Code of Business Conduct," https://tinyurl.com/yakw8xtt, accessed April 21, 2020, 18.

22.   CFA Institute, "Code of Ethics and Standards of Professional Conduct," https://tinyurl.com/uh83u2s, accessed April 30, 2020.

23.   J. Kaplan, "The Conflict of Interest Blog," https://tinyurl.com/ya7yh6l2, accessed April 21, 2020.

24.   Verizon, "Code of Conduct," https://tinyurl.com/y8yqs6p2, accessed April 21, 2020, 15.

25.   Verizon, "Code of Conduct," 27.

26.   Verizon, "Code of Conduct," 15.

27.   Mastercard, "Code of Conduct 2017," personal archives, 5.

28.   Mastercard, "Code of Conduct," 7.

29. Mastercard, "Code of Conduct," 7.

30. Mastercard, "Code of Conduct," 9.

31. Citibank, "Code of Conduct," https://tinyurl.com/y7sf9w8t, accessed April 21, 2020, 20–23.

32. Citibank, "Description of Citi's EMEA Conflicts of Interest Policy," https://tinyurl.com/y8hp3mnu, accessed April 21, 2020.

33. Citibank, "Code of Conduct," https://tinyurl.com/y7sf9w8t, accessed April 21, 2020.

BIBLIOGRAPHY

Altman, M. C. "The Decomposition of the Corporate Body: What Kant Cannot Contribute to Business Ethics." *Journal of Business Ethics* 74 (2007): 253–266.

Aristotle. *Metaphysics*. Translated by Hippocrates G. Apostle. Des Moines, IA: The Peripatetic Press, 1979.

———. *Nicomachean Ethics*. Translated by J. Sachs. Newburyport, MA: Focus Publishing, 2011.

Benson, G. C. S. "Codes of Ethics." *Journal of Business Ethics* 8 (1989): 305–319.

Bentham, J. *The Principles of Morals and Legislation*. Amherst, NY: Prometheus, 1988.

Boatright, J. R. "Conflict of Interest: An Agency Analysis." In *Ethics and Agency Theory*, edited by N. Bowie and R. E. Freeman, 187–203. Oxford: Oxford University Press, 1992.

———. "Conflict of Interest." In *Encyclopedia of Business Ethics and Society*, vol. 1, edited by R. W. Kolb, 400–404. Los Angeles: SAGE Publications, 2008.

Bowie, N. E. *Business Ethics: A Kantian Perspective*. Malden, MA: Blackwell, 1999.

Cain, D. M., G. Loewenstein, and D. A. Moore. "Coming Clean but Playing Dirtier: The Shortcomings of Disclosure as a Solution to Conflicts of Interest." In *Conflicts of Interest: Challenges and Solutions in Business, Law, Medicine, and Public Policy*, edited by D. A. Moore, D. M. Cain, G. Loewenstein, and M. H. Bazerman, 104–125. New York: Cambridge University Press, 2005.

Carson, T. L. "Conflicts of Interest." *Journal of Business Ethics* 13 (1994): 387–404.

———. "Conflicts of Interest and Self-Dealing in the Professions: A Review Essay." *Business Ethics Quarterly* 14, no. 1 (2004): 161–182.

Crisp, R. *Mill on Utilitarianism*. London: Routledge, 2001.

Davis, M. "Conflict of Interest." *Business & Professional Ethics Journal* 1, no. 4 (1982): 17–27.

———. "Conflict of Interest Revisited." *Business & Professional Ethics Journal* 12, no. 4 (1993): 21–41.

———. "Introduction." In *Conflicts of Interest in the Professions*, edited by M. Davis and A. Stark, 3–19. Oxford: Oxford University Press, 2001.

―――. "Conflict of Interest." In *Encyclopedia of Applied Ethics*, vol. 1, second edition, edited by R. Chadwick, D. Callahan, and P. Singer, 571–577. Amsterdam: Elsevier, 2012.

Freeman, R. E. "Managing for Stakeholders." In *Ethical Theory and Business*, ninth edition, edited by D. G. Arnold, T. L. Beauchamp, and N. E. Bowie, 57–68. Boston: Pearson, 2013.

Friedman, M. *Capitalism and Freedom*. Chicago: University of Chicago Press, 1962.

―――. "The Social Responsibility of Business is to Increase its Profits." In *Ethical Theory and Business*, ninth edition, edited by D. G. Arnold, T. L. Beauchamp, and N. E. Bowie, 53–57. Boston: Pearson, 2013. For the online version of the original publication, see https://graphics8.nytimes.com/packages/pdf/business/miltonfriedman1970.pdf.

Ibañez, F. "A Necessary Ethics Definition for Conflicts of Interest" (working title). *Business & Professional Ethics Journal* (forthcoming).

Kant, I. *Grounding for the Metaphysics of Morals*. Translated by J. W. Ellington. Indianapolis, IN: Hackett, 1993.

―――. *Critique of Pure Reason*. Translated by P. Guyer and A. Wood. Cambridge: Cambridge University Press, 1999.

―――. *Critique of the Power of Judgment*. Translated by P. Guyer and E. Matthews. Cambridge: Cambridge University Press, 2000.

―――. *Critique of Practical Reason*. Translated by M. Gregor. Cambridge: Cambridge University Press, 2015.

Kaptein, M. and M. S. Schwartz. "The Effectiveness of Business Codes: A Critical Examination of Existing Studies and the Development of an Integrated Research Model." *Journal of Business Ethics* 77 (2008): 111–127.

Kierkegaard, S. *Either/or: A Fragment of Life*. Translated by A. Hannay. London: Penguin Books, 1992.

Kotler, P. and N. Lee. *Corporate Social Responsibility: Doing the Most Good for Your Company and Your Cause*. Hoboken, NJ: John Wiley & Sons 2005.

Lewis, C. S. *The Abolition of Man*. New York: Harper, 2000.

Luebke, N. R. "Conflict of Interest as a Moral Category." *Business & Professional Ethics Journal* 6, no. 1 (1987): 66–81.

MacAskill, W. *Doing Good Better*. New York: Penguin Random House, 2015.

Melé, D. "Corporate Social Responsibility Theories." In *The Oxford Handbook of Corporate Social Responsibility*, edited by A. Crane, A. McWilliams, D. Matten, J. Moon, and D. S. Stegel, 55–62. Oxford: Oxford University Press, 2008.

Mill, J. S. "On Liberty." In *John Stuart Mill: On Liberty and Other Essays*, edited by J. Gray, 5–128. Oxford: Oxford University Press, 1991.

―――. "The Subjection of Women." In *John Stuart Mill: On Liberty and Other Essays*, edited by J. Gray, 469–582. Oxford: Oxford University Press, 1991.

―――. *Utilitarianism and the 1868 Speech on Capital Punishment*. Edited by G. Sher. Indianapolis, IN: Hackett Publishing Company, 2001.

Nietzsche, F. *On the Genealogy of Morals*. Translated by D. Smith. Oxford: Oxford University Press, 2008.

Norman, W. and C. MacDonald. "Conflicts of Interest." In *The Oxford Handbook of Business Ethics*, edited by G. G. Brenkert, and T. L. Beauchamp, 441–470. New York: Oxford University Press, 2010.

Oxford University Press. *A Dictionary of Finance and Banking*. Oxford: Oxford University Press, 1998.

Pence, G. *A Dictionary of Common Philosophical Terms*. New York: The McGraw-Hill Companies, 2000.

Plato. *Republic*. Translated by A. Bloom. New York: Basic Books, 1991.

———. *Five Dialogues. Euthyphro, Apology, Crito, Meno, Phaedo*. Translated by G. M. A. Grupe and reviewed by J. M. Cooper. Indianapolis, IN: Hackett, 2002.

Pritchard, M. "Conflicts of Interest: Conceptual and Normative Issues." *Academic Medicine* 71, no. 12 (1996): 1305–1313.

Sandel, M. *Justice. What's the Right Thing to Do?* New York: Farrar, Straus and Giroux, 2009.

———. *What Money Can't Buy: The Moral Limits of Markets*. New York: Farrar, Straus and Giroux, 2013.

Schwab, A. B. "Defining Conflicts of Interest in Terms of Judgment." *Business and Professional Ethics Journal* 38, no. 1 (2019): 111–131.

Singer, P. *The Life You Can Save*. New York: Random House, 2010.

Stark, A. "Comparing Conflicts of Interest Across the Professions." In *Conflict of Interest in the Professions*, edited by M. Davis and A. Stark, 335–351. Oxford: Oxford University Press, 2001.

Stigand, W. *The Life, Work, and Opinions of Heinrich Heine*. Volume 1. London: Longmans, Green & Co., 1875.

Villarán, A. "Conflicts of Interest: A Moral Analysis." *Business & Professional Ethics Journal* 39, no. 1 (2020): 121–142.

Wike, V. S. *Kant on Happiness in Ethics*. New York: SUNY Press, 1994.

INDEX